Plays for Clowns in Christ

OPEN 7

Plays for Clowns in Christ

Four Short Plays for the Fun of Playing!!

by

RICHARD URDAHL

FORTRESS PRESS • PHILADELPHIA

Library of Congress Catalogue Card Number 72–91527

ISBN 0–8006–0145–9

3474H72   Printed in U.S.A.   1-145

Prologue

Some people find it difficult to laugh in church—especially preachers. The joy of worship is too often austere rather than open and free. The healing that comes from a hearty laugh is usually reserved for parties. But why not holy hilarity? Why not a joyous banquet with jokes, celebrations, and jesters? Why not a comedy for the Lord? Why not be clowns for Christ when the time is right? Fools for Christ, is what Paul calls Christians. That designation, alas, has been a subject for serious sermons rather than a clue for our life style or our worship style.

Yet the clown in each of us yearns to laugh and ease the tensions of our fear and doubt. The hidden humor of Jesus' parables, the satire of the biblical proverbs, and the hilarious antics of men like Jacob and David are but a few precedents from the Scriptures that enable us to hear the truth ring through slapstick, comedy, and smiles. Richard Urdahl helps us do the same thing with his plays. They are almost like chancel cartoons. They are surely for clowns in Christ. His play, "What Are We Going to Do With All These Rotting Fish?" published in Open Book 4 was a roaring success . . . and a big laugh! Now Urdahl offers us four more, none of which is quite the same. But each reflects his fresh and fun-filled approach to religious drama. He brings us to our knees with our own folly. He helps us laugh at ourselves. His plays, like many of the medieval morality plays, let the ludicrous and foolish ways of men come to the surface. They are for free fools, for clowns in Christ, for people who dare to look in the mirror and laugh and laugh and laugh. And with that laughter comes a new beginning. Let each play be that wherever you perform it.

How should plays like this be presented? There are no holds barred. The freedom and fun of these plays invite you to stage them as you wish. Here the chancel and the circus have much in common. When the spirit of these plays comes through there will be joy in heaven. Here is a chance to let your hair down and bring the house down. As the author himself says of the plays, "I am reluctant to tell you what to do with these plays, even though a number of people have told me what to do with them. I wish only to say that they are largely vehicles for entertaining, so I urge you not to impute to them alien intentions. If you want to do profound stuff, please look elsewhere. But if you think that there are redemptive possibilities within laughter, you might find these plays useful. A final word: don't be afraid to change words, delete phrases, rewrite passages, and generally refurbish these plays. They need all the help you can give them." With that word there is nothing more to say, except, it's play time!

Norman Habel
Editor of Open Books

The Plays in This Book

If I'm the Last, You're in Trouble

A chancel drama

Production Notes

1) Telephone—The telephone can be real or imaginary; in either case the voices can be recorded on
   tape (cassette is preferable because of its size);
   the ring of the telephone can be similarly taped;
   a third person must be concealed as close to the
   telephone as possible, e.g., in or behind a pulpit
   or specially draped table; when done carefully,
   the voices can be taped from regular telephone
   conversation; it is imperative that the telephone
   voices be heard, hence volume and fidelity must
   be checked in the church/auditorium/room where
   the play is to be presented.

2) Voice—After the Voice is heard on the telephone,
   it can be heard on a regular P.A. system or the
   speaker for Voice may be in choir loft, if acous-
   tics permit, or some concealed spot that is suffi-
   ciently distant from Bert.

3) Shot—It should sound as much like a gun shot,
   really, shots, as possible; they can be on the same
   tape as the telephone conversation; it is perhaps
   more effective to have someone, e.g., Voice in loft,
   to fire a pistol with blanks or a starter's pistol.

Characters

ETHELBERT SMYTHE (alias BERT SMITH)
THE VOICE OF GOD
MOTHER-ON-THE-TELEPHONE

Time

Hopefully not, but probably, now.

Setting

Bert's apartment in The Loving Arms On-the-Knoll-
by-the-Bluff.

If I'm the Last, You're in Trouble

[BERT, *returning from work, enters his apartment; he's holding the day's mail, which he places on a table as he takes off his coat and hat; he then returns to the table and picks up one of the letters; it is very large and attractive; purple in color.*]

BERT: What a magnificent envelope! Let me see, I'll bet that it's either from BankAmericard or the Reader's Digest! [*Opens envelope and reads letter silently; does double take.*] UPON RECEIPT OF THIS LETTER, PLEASE PHONE THIS NUMBER IMMEDIATELY. ZENITH 33333. URGENT NEWS. LOVE. GOD. [*Rereads letter to himself.*] What kind of sick mind would write this? It's obscene! It's a moral outrage! I'm going to take it to the Postmaster! No, I'd better report this directly to the F.B.I.! [*Telephone rings; he answers it bruskly.*] Hello!

VOICE: I've been awaiting your call.

BERT: I beg your pardon?

VOICE: Kindly reread the letter you're holding in your left hand.

BERT [*quickly placing hand behind his back*]: What are you talking about?

VOICE: The letter you're now holding behind your back.

BERT: What letter? [*Lets it fall to the floor.*]

VOICE: The one you just dropped.

BERT: Now listen, wise guy . . . I don't know what your game is but I've had enough of your stupid jokes! You may be too sick to know it . . . but there are laws against obscene letters and crank phone calls! I'm warning you . . . you need help and you need it badly! You'd better see a doctor . . . or a priest! Believe me, you are one sick cookie!

VOICE: COOKIE?

BERT: I'm hanging up now . . . and let me warn you! If you phone once again I'll have the call traced and you'll be in real, big trouble! Understand? Goodbye! [*Hangs up; picks up letter, gingerly, and places it on the table.*] Well, that's that, dummy! Talk about sick! But . . . it's all over now.

VOICE: On the contrary!

BERT [*looking around room for the source of the VOICE*]: What the. . . .

VOICE: Do not think that you can elude me thus easily. You? Elude me? You? Flee from my presence? Where? El Paso? I am there! Bangor? I am there! Take the wings of the morning and dwell in Pasadena? I am there.

BERT [*shaking head in disbelief*]: Well, I'll be da. . . .

VOICE: You may well be! But I'LL decide that!

BERT [*laughing nervously*]: You mean that . . . that . . . you really are. . . .

VOICE: I AM.

BERT: Really?

VOICE: I AM.

BERT: Well, I'll be . . . blessed!

VOICE: That too is MY decision!

BERT: Oh, my God. . . .

VOICE: Yes?

BERT: I need a drink . . . of water, just water, I only drink water. . . .

VOICE: What a pity.

BERT: This is too much!

VOICE: I don't understand you.

BERT: Well . . . you'll have to admit that this . . . this whole business is a little . . . a little spooky!

VOICE: Spooky? Couldn't you have said "far out"? And whose fault is it? It was I who tried the normal channels of communication. I wrote. I phoned. But, oh, no, you would have nothing to do with them! You would have nothing to do with a "sick cookie"!

BERT [*convicted*]: I . . . I . . . I am a man of unclean lips!

VOICE: I've heard that before.

BERT: I am the chief of sinners! I am. . . .

VOICE: Before you lay the whited-sepulcher bit on me. . . .

BERT: DUNG! But I believe. I do believe . . . [VOICE *has anticipated following line and speaks it with him.*] . . . help thou my unbelief! [*He drops to his knees in contrite prayer, folded hands, bowed head, etc.*]

VOICE: Oh, come off it! I want to talk but you want to be pious!

BERT: But I'm bringing forth fruit worthy of repentance!

VOICE: Then LISTEN to me.

BERT [*standing up*]: Oh, I'm listening! And let me apologize for not believing your letter . . . and the phone call . . . and your desire to use regular, normal, ordinary forms of communication. And I am going to listen to you now . . . HOWEVER. . . .

VOICE: Yes?

BERT: In order that our conversation can be as normal and ordinary as possible . . . I want that as much as you do . . . so. . . .

VOICE: So?

BERT: . . . so just appear here before me . . . right here . . . now. That way our conversation would be so much more REAL . . . and MEANINGFUL.

VOICE: Isn't my voice real?

BERT: Yes.

VOICE: Isn't it meaningful?

BERT: Yes, but. . . .

VOICE: But what?

BERT: This is the twentieth century! An age of personalism! Personal conversation, personal encounters, personal this, personal that, personal property, personal ethics, personal EVERYTHING!

VOICE: So?

BERT: A voice . . . just a voice . . . is not all that personal!

VOICE: Not personal? A voice? Not personal? Think, man, think! What is more real, more meaningful, more moving than two people together in the aloneness of darkness . . . the realest touch they

7

experience are whispered words of love. And remember: Death is not the stilled heart. It is the
stilled voice.

BERT: May I speak frankly?

VOICE: I listen to no other kind of speaking.

BERT: This is the twentieth century, an age of HON-
ESTY [VOICE *coughs loudly*] . . . God bless you . . .
and honesty compels me to tell you that poetry and
aphorisms, however beautiful and profound, are
nonetheless the last refuge of the effete!

VOICE: Effete! Anyway, since you don't seem to know
that the word is an adjective, not a noun, I doubt
that you know what the word means!

BERT: Effete: exhausted of vitality, force, or effec-
tiveness; depleted of vigor; worn out; spent.

VOICE: So, your superior intelligence has led you to
conclude that I am exhausted, depleted, and spent
. . . simply because I refuse to corporealize. . . .

BERT: Corporealize?

VOICE: Look it up, look it up . . . simply because I
refuse to play, "And now . . . here's Jehovah!"

BERT [*shouting*]: That's not what I meant! [*Realiz-
ing he's shouting at God*] Excuse me . . . please
. . . I didn't mean to shout. [*Nearly whispering*]
I'm really very sorry. [*Beating his chest liturgically*]
I'm a sinner, a super son of a . . . sinner.

8

VOICE: Then what *did* you mean?

BERT: I simply meant that . . . that . . . I've forgotten what I meant.

VOICE: Listen, what would have happened if I had assumed a body? I would have walked into this room, greeted you, identified myself, and tried to engage you in conversation. But what would you have done?

BERT: Fainted?

VOICE: You? A twentieth-century man . . . faint in the presence of God? Fat chance! You would have said, "Do something zingy! Make yourself invisible! Do this, do that, give me this, give me that. Turn water into rye!

BERT [*loudly*]: Now just a minute . . . [*softly*] . . . if I may put it that way . . . I thought that miracles were your big shtick! After all, I've read the bible from cover to cover. . . .

VOICE: Bully for you.

BERT: . . . and without miracles . . . well, really, without them you just wouldn't have made it.

VOICE: Made it? Made it where?

BERT: Why, to the top, of course!

VOICE: The top of what?

9

BERT [*reflective pause*]: Oh . . . ya . . . I guess I forgot about that. [*Brief pause.*] O.K. . . . let's talk! You mentioned in your letter that you had an urgent message for me. I hope it isn't bad news! [*Crosses his fingers.*] I'm ready. Shoot.

VOICE: I'm here to inform you that. . . .

BERT: I know that I've done things I should not have done. . . .

VOICE: I'm here to. . . .

BERT: . . . and not done things I should have done. . . .

VOICE: . . . to tell you that you. . . .

BERT: . . . I am chief of sinners. . . .

VOICE: . . . are THE LAST CHRISTIAN ON EARTH!

BERT: . . . unworthy to tie your sandals . . . I'M WHAT?

VOICE: The last. . . .

BERT: Christian?

VOICE: . . . on earth!

BERT [*very rapidly*]: I'm the last Christian on earth?

VOICE [*equally fast*]: You're the last Christian on earth!

BERT [*laughingly*]: You can't be serious!

VOICE: I CAN'T?

BERT: You can.

VOICE: I am!

BERT: You are! But . . . there have to be more!

VOICE: There aren't.

BERT: You've really looked everywhere?

VOICE: From California to the New York island!

BERT: And the churches . . . you've tried ALL the churches?

VOICE: All of them.

BERT: Hey, what about seminaries!

VOICE: You've got to be kidding!

BERT: The Pope! You forgot the Pope!

VOICE: No.

BERT: But there's always Billy Graham!

VOICE: No.

BERT: Do you realize what you are saying?

VOICE: You are the last Christian on earth!

BERT: I hate to say this . . . I really do . . . but if I'm the last, you're in real trouble!

VOICE: Oh?

BERT: Real, real trouble.

VOICE: I am?

BERT: I hate to do this . . . I really do . . . I hate to kick a guy when he's down . . . believe me, I know how low you must feel . . . abandoned by your friends . . . betrayed by those you counted on . . . but there's something I've got to tell you . . . and it's going to hurt you more than it does me.

VOICE: Yes?

BERT: If you're pinning your hopes on me . . . tough luck, I. . . .

VOICE: You?

BERT: I hate to be the one who has to tell you. . . .

VOICE: Tell me what?

BERT: . . . that I . . . I am NOT a Christian.

VOICE: Oh.

BERT: Oh? Is that all you've got to say. Didn't you hear me?

VOICE: I heard you.

BERT: But don't you realize what my words meant? They meant that there are no more Christians on earth!

VOICE: Wrong.

BERT: Well, name just one!

VOICE: You.

BERT: But I am not a Christian!

VOICE: You are.

BERT: You don't know what you're saying!

VOICE: Dare you argue with Omniscience himself?

BERT: When you put it that way . . . no! I admit that I don't know very much . . . in spite of my B.A. . . . but I do know myself!

VOICE: How Socratic.

BERT: Thank you.

VOICE: Hence, you know you are a Christian.

13

BERT: Listen . . . I'll at least give you this . . . at one time or another I may have been a Christian . . . but who hasn't! Now? No way.

VOICE: Wrong again.

BERT: This is absurd! If I'm an example of what it means to be a Christian, I'd sure as . . . hades hate to see a non-Christian! Think it over! You're better off without me . . . without US!

VOICE: Who are you to rewrite my plans?

BERT: All right, I'll tell you! I'm a fellow, just a fellow BUT a fellow who hates to see anyone make a fool of himself!

VOICE: You think I am a FOOL?

BERT: Yes!

[*Sound of a "shot"; BERT cringes and falls to the floor.*]

VOICE: Oh, come off it! That was just a tired, old Chevy with dirty points!

BERT: It wasn't one of your. . . .

VOICE: I told you before . . . I'm more interested in conversation than games!

BERT [*stands up*]: O.K. . . . but, first, let me make myself perfectly clear! I apologize for what I said. You're not a fool!

14

VOICE: That is your HONEST conviction?

BERT [*long pause*]: Ah . . . no, it isn't. But at least you're not an ordinary fool!

VOICE: I'm an EXTRAORDINARY fool?

BERT: Yes, I mean, NO! I don't know what I mean! And would you please stop brutalizing me!

VOICE: Brutalizing?

BERT: Look it up, look it up! For the last time, I am not a Christian!

VOICE: You are.

BERT: But I am not hungering and thirsting after righteousness!

VOICE: Yes, you are.

BERT: Then it's a very low-level hunger pang!

VOICE: That you DON'T have to tell me.

BERT: And I shouldn't have to tell you that I'm not. . . .

VOICE: But you are!

BERT: Then it's all over!

VOICE: I'll decide when it's over!

BERT: I'm not a Christian!

VOICE: You are!

BERT: And you're an extraordinary fool!

VOICE: I named you my own!

BERT: When?

VOICE: At your baptism.

BERT: But I was just a baby!

VOICE: I wasn't!

BERT: I didn't even know what was happening!

VOICE: I did!

BERT: But I renounced that action!

VOICE: But you haven't!

BERT: You are a bully!

VOICE: I am not!

BERT: But you are forcing me to. . . .

VOICE: I'm not forcing you to do a thing!

BERT: But you're shouting!

VOICE: The TRUTH! I feel strongly about the TRUTH. You are the last. You are mine.

BERT [*desperately*]: I am not yours, I am not yours . . . I refuse you, I renounce you, I denounce you . . . I . . . I spit on you! [*He spits.*]

VOICE [*pause*]: You missed! [BERT *spits in different directions.*] Oh, come, now . . . enough of that!

16

BERT [*again realizing what he has done*]: What have I done? Believe me, I'm sorry, I'm sorry . . . forgive me, please forgive me . . . I didn't mean to. . . .

VOICE: Of course, you did.

BERT: I didn't!

VOICE: You did. But. . . .

BERT [*fearfully*]: BUT?

VOICE: You missed. So, let's get on with. . . .

BERT: You're not going to punish me?

VOICE: Why should I do that?

BERT: Because I tried to. . . .

VOICE: You were angry at me.

BERT: So?

VOICE: So what?

BERT: So punish me!

VOICE: But I'm not angry at you.

BERT: You MUST punish me!

VOICE: Come, now, we've more important things to do. . . .

BERT: You must punish me! I can't stand it!

VOICE: You can't stand what?

17

BERT: Not being punished!

VOICE: You ARE a twentieth-century man!

BERT: I must be PUNISHED!

VOICE: Very well, IF you insist that I do something. . . .

BERT: I do! [*Closes eyes, clenches fists, preparing for the worst.*]

VOICE: All right, here goes! I forgive you! Now, we've finished with that!

BERT [*incredulously*]: You FORGIVE me?

VOICE: That's right.

BERT: To be forgiven . . . that's PUNISHMENT?

VOICE: For a twentieth-century man it evidently is!

BERT: I thought so . . . you are SICK! I want to be punished!

VOICE: For the love of pete, who's sick? You try to spit on me, you beg me to forgive you, I forgive you . . . then you say "No! Beat me!" THAT'S mental health! ? ! ? If it's beating you want, well . . . go beat yourself!

BERT: Come on, now . . . I haven't done that since I was a kid.

VOICE: Oh, me! I'm afraid I'm backing another loser!

BERT: So don't back me!

VOICE: So don't tempt me!

BERT: You see! You do want to punish me . . . maybe even KILL me!

VOICE: Lead me not into temptation!

[*Telephone rings;* BERT *pauses; then rushes to phone, answering brusquely.*]

BERT: Hello!

MOTHER [*slight pause*]: Ethelbert? Is that you?

BERT: Of course, it's me, mother. Now what do you want?

MOTHER: Ethelbert, is something wrong?

BERT: No, nothing's wrong, nothing's wrong . . . so what is it?

MOTHER: Something IS wrong! You can't fool me! A mother always. . . .

BERT: NOTHING is wrong! I'm just . . . very busy!

MOTHER: Too busy to talk to your very own mother?

BERT: All right . . . I'm sorry. I didn't mean to be rude. . . .

MOTHER: That's not like you at all!

BERT: Mother, please! I'm . . . I'm occupied at the moment!

19

MOTHER: You're not alone?

BERT: Yes . . . and NO!

MOTHER: Whatever are you saying? Ethelbert Smythe! Do you have a WOMAN in your apartment?

BERT: Of course not!

MOTHER: That's nice. But who IS there?

BERT: I'll phone you later!

MOTHER: It IS a woman!

BERT: Mother! It is not a woman! I'm talking to . . . to a very famous . . . AUTHOR!

MOTHER: Oh, how exciting! Who is it?

BERT: Mother, I have to. . . .

MOTHER: What book did he write?

BERT: I've forgotten . . . he's written so many!

MOTHER: Well, you can at least name one!

BERT: EXODUS!

MOTHER: Leon Uris! You're talking with Leon Uris? My Ethelbert . . . talking with. . . .

BERT: I've got to go now.

MOTHER: But promise me you'll get his autograph!

BERT: Goodbye, mother. . . .

MOTHER: Just a minute, Ethelbert, one more item. The church secretary phoned me. She's been trying to contact you for weeks. It's been over three years since you communed or contributed anything, so unless you do something about it, they're taking you off the church roster.

BERT: Fine! I've GOT to go now!

MOTHER: Did you say FINE! ? ! ?

BERT: Yes, mother, goodbye, mother.

MOTHER: But don't you want to be a Christian?

BERT: It's funny you should ask that!

MOTHER: Well, son, you know it's up to you. I've done all I can! You're a big boy now. No one's going to twist your arm! The decision is yours! But . . . I think it'd be nice if you sent the church ten dollars. Then I'm sure they'd forget the communion requirement!

BERT: I'll send a check today!

MOTHER: That's nice. And, Ethelbert. . . .

BERT: Yes, mother?

MOTHER: Don't forget the autograph!

BERT: No, mother, goodbye, mother!

MOTHER: And ask Leon what he thinks of PORT-NOY'S COMPLAINT! I think it's perfectly HOR-RIBLE! No son of mine would do those. . . .

BERT: Goodbye, mother! [*He hangs up; speaks to* VOICE.] That was mother.

VOICE: Indeed. And would you like me to tell you what she's saying now?

BERT: You leave my mother out of this!

VOICE: Joyfully.

BERT: But I hope you listened to her! She said it was up to me whether or not I want to remain a Christian. It is MY decision! My mother said that!

VOICE: Mother erred!

BERT: Can't anyone say NO to you?

VOICE: Of course. And everyone else has!

BERT: I say NO!

VOICE: But you can't.

BERT: WHY can't I?

VOICE: I'm as puzzled by that as you are.

BERT: But others have said NO!

VOICE: And MEANT it!

BERT: Then I say NO, NO, NO, NO!

VOICE: But you don't mean it!

BERT: I do!

VOICE: You don't! If you did, I wouldn't be here!

BERT: Believe me, I am saying NO!

VOICE: And you believe me! You are NOT saying NO!

BERT: It's not fair! You won't believe me!

VOICE: I cannot believe a lie!

BERT: This is ridiculous!

VOICE: That thought has occurred to me too!

BERT: You're trying to brainwash me!

VOICE: Impossible!

BERT: Then I'm going crazy!

VOICE: What makes you think that?

BERT: Well. . . .

VOICE: Well?

BERT: Just listen to me!

VOICE: I am.

BERT: That's what I mean! I really think that I'm talking to God!

VOICE: That's not so crazy. Isn't it crazier to think of God talking to YOU?

BERT: Then we're BOTH crazy!

VOICE: That doesn't follow!

BERT: Why are you doing this to me?

Voice: Doing what?

Bert: Humiliating me!

Voice: Humiliating you?

Bert: That's right!

Voice: I tell you that you are NOT crazy and that humiliates you?

Bert: Absolutely!

Voice: You're crazy, man!

Bert: You see, you see! You DO think I'm crazy!

Voice: Don't be such a literalist!

Bert [*deep sigh*]: I . . . I'm tired . . . beat! I need a drink . . . for my stomach's sake, of course!

Voice: Your stomach's sake? Why, oh why, did St. Paul ever use that old ruse! Wine is NOT for the tummy. It's for the SPIRIT! If you're sick, take two aspirin!

Bert: You know . . . this is all so crazy . . . so mind-boggling . . . that it must be true! It must be true!

Voice: Now you're talking like a first-century man!

Bert: But tell me? What went wrong?

Voice: What do you mean?

Bert: Well, I have a pretty strong hunch that you

never planned that *I* was going to be the last Christian! Did you?

VOICE: I . . . I . . . I'd rather not answer that question.

BERT: Just think . . . I . . . Ethelbert Smythe . . . the LAST of a noble race! But, you know . . . maybe this is not so strange after all! As I remember it . . . and I haven't thought about it for a long time . . . I was really a very faithful confirmand! Except during the baseball season. . . .

VOICE: Friend. . . .

BERT: . . . and . . . ah, it's all coming back to me . . . I was a pretty snappy altar boy . . . and if it weren't for that episode with the communion wine . . . but you know that I didn't drink ALL of it . . . but I couldn't rat on my buddies . . . I'm no Judas! And then. . . .

VOICE: Friend. . . .

BERT: I was considering the ministry . . . really and truly considering it . . . until that guidance counselor told me about salary-schedules . . . not that I worship money . . . certainly not now. . . .

VOICE: Friend. . . .

BERT: So all things considered. . . .

VOICE: FRIEND!

BERT: Yes?

VOICE: Last does NOT, repeat, does NOT, mean BEST NOR TRUEST NOR NOBLEST NOR FAITHFULLEST!

BERT: It doesn't?

VOICE: Last means LAST! That's all. O.K.?

BERT: Did I . . . did I appear to be . . . bragging?

VOICE: Let's just say that you were taking the long road toward . . . humility.

BERT: If you say so that's O.K. with me. And forgive me for doubting you! You were right all along! I AM the LAST CHRISTIAN on earth! So. . . .

VOICE: So?

BERT: So let's get busy! I'm rarin' to go! LAST IS FAST! You shout the orders and I'll obey! We're a TEAM now! God and Ethelbert! Wait and see . . . I may even convince you that last is best! When, where, and how do I start?

VOICE: That's up. . . .

BERT: I bet I know! [*Preachy*] Listen, you generations of vipers! The world is coming to its end! You are all doomed! So repent and believe or . . . [*dropping preachy tone*] I can't do THAT! Someone MIGHT repent and believe and then I wouldn't be the LAST! I'd better forget the call for repentance . . . I'll just say. . . .

VOICE: Why couldn't you have been a Trappist monk?

BERT: What's that?

VOICE: You wouldn't understand.

BERT: Maybe not now . . . but I'll learn fast and what I learn I'll not forget. Say, I just thought of something: You know what the problem was . . . with my predecessors, I mean? Too many hypocrites! No wonder you gave them the ol' heave-ho!

VOICE: They gave ME the ol' heave-ho!

BERT: Well, that won't happen again! But, I'm talking too much . . . let's get with it . . . what do I do?

VOICE: That's up to you.

BERT: What's up to me?

VOICE: What you decide to do!

BERT: What *I* decide to do?

VOICE: That's right.

BERT: Well . . . it's true that I've got a few good ideas . . . and I'm toying with some others . . . but you'll have to give me a few pointers . . . at least, to begin with! So, when do I start?

VOICE: Now.

BERT: Right! And what do I do?

28

VOICE: Whatever you think appropriate.

BERT: Just a minute . . . I'm afraid I'm not making myself clear. . . .

VOICE: On the contrary!

BERT: I'm a little short on experience . . . I mean, I've never been the last Christian on earth before! So, what's the plan?

VOICE: It's up to you.

BERT: But in the letter you said that you had something to tell me!

VOICE: And I've told you.

BERT: You've told me what?

VOICE: The message.

BERT: All you've told me is that I'm the last Christian on earth!

VOICE: That's. . . .

BERT: The message?

VOICE: . . . the message.

BERT: You HAVE to be joking!

VOICE: *I* do not HAVE to do anything! I may CHOOSE to do something . . . and it's done! Do you understand?

BERT: I understand . . . I think.

VOICE: Good. Now, I am leaving.

BERT: But you CAN'T leave!

VOICE: CAN'T!

BERT: You can leave, you can leave, you can do anything you want, but PLEASE don't leave, not yet!

VOICE: But you have the message.

BERT: I have it.

VOICE: And you believe it.

BERT: I believe it.

VOICE: Goodbye, then.

BERT: NO! NOT YET! PLEASE, NOT YET!

VOICE: I am going. I've already spent more time with you than I did with Abraham or Moses.

BERT: That may be . . . but look what happened to them!

VOICE: What happened to them?

BERT: If you'd spent more time with them they wouldn't have failed you!

VOICE: Failed me? Abraham and Moses failed me? Failed me?

BERT: Well. . . .

VOICE: Well?

BERT: Well, for one thing, they never became Christians, did they?

VOICE [*after long pause*]: Will you do me a favor?

BERT: Anything . . . just name it!

VOICE: Renounce me!

BERT: What?

VOICE: Denounce me!

BERT: Do what?

VOICE: In your heart of hearts . . . curse me!

BERT: I can't do that! I won't do that! I am the LAST Christian on this earth!

VOICE: Goody.

BERT: Hey, wait a minute! I know what you're doing? You're TESTING me!

VOICE: And you, me! I will now say goodbye and . . . good luck!

BERT: I still need your help!

VOICE: There are others with whom I must speak.

BERT: Others? Then I'm NOT the LAST ONE! I was afraid this would happen! All along I've had the hunch that this was all just one big colossal trick!

VOICE: Trick?

BERT: Or TACTIC . . . if that sounds better! Sure, go around to "x" number of Christians . . . and tell each of them . . . oh, so convincingly . . . that he is the last of the breed . . . your last hope!

VOICE: My last hope?

BERT: I've got to hand it to you, it's not a bad plan. Say the right words and you can move mountains . . . turn us all into heroes . . . get us to tithe . . . and all because we think we're the last! So . . . never mind if the whole deal is a little . . . shady.

VOICE: Shady?

BERT: . . . ambiguous, then . . . but who cares if it's morally ambiguous because it'll get the job done! Right? Why, just look at me! A half-hour ago I was a nothing . . . a theological drop-out! But now look at me! I'm THE DEFINITIVE CHRISTIAN!

VOICE: NOT definitive! Just LAST!

BERT: But didn't you just tell me that you had to leave me and go talk with someone else?

VOICE: I did.

BERT: But how can you do that IF I'm the last Christian on earth?

VOICE: Do you think that I talk ONLY to Christians? Is my commerce among my Creation thus limited?

BERT: Well, I . . . I suppose not. But IF there are others. . . .

VOICE: There ARE!

BERT: . . . then that means that I'm just not all that important.

VOICE: Not all that important? How can you say that? Remember . . . never forget that there is no name that speaks mine so completely as yours!

BERT: Mine? ? ? Ethelbert Smythe? ! ? !

VOICE: THE NAME IS "CHRISTIAN"! CHRIST'S MAN! [*Pause*] Ethelbert Smythe? ? ? Let me give you a new name. [*Pause*] Bert Smith! Bert Smith, Christian!

BERT [*listening to the sound of the new name*]: Bert Smith . . . Bert . . . I like that! No frills . . . it's . . . lean . . . and powerful! Bert Smith, Lean and Powerful! Bert Smith, the last Christian on the earth!

VOICE: Now, I MUST leave.

BERT: Wait a minute . . . WAIT A MINUTE [*having thought of something*] . . . wait a minute, wait a minute, wait a minute! About this "last" business? When you think about it . . . I mean REALLY think about it . . . I may BE the last, but I cannot REMAIN the last! Last DOESN'T mean . . . THE END! It really means the BEGIN-NING, doesn't it?

VOICE: Maybe I'd better wait a moment or two. . . .

BERT: THAT'S IT!

VOICE: . . . or three. . . .

BERT: I've got it!

VOICE: . . . or four. . . .

BERT [*very excited*]: LISTEN TO THIS!

VOICE: . . . or more!

BERT: Check this out: if I am what I am . . . then as others see me and talk with me . . . they may want to become what I am . . . since what I am is what I AM is! Right? Great God Almighty! Why, this is like . . . PENTECOST! I'm saying things even I don't understand! ! !

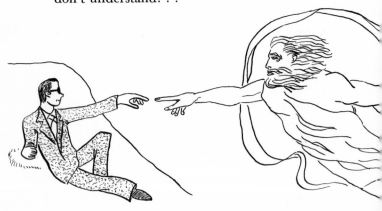

VOICE: Well, there is at least the rushing of a mighty wind! !

BERT: I'm NOT the last! I'm the FIRST Christian on the earth . . . NOW! THE FIRST! That's even better! If you'll excuse me, I've got work to do! I've got to get busy, busy, busy!

VOICE: Please, not TOO busy!

BERT: Don't worry . . . I'm evolving a PLAN!

VOICE: Dare I ask what it is?

BERT: NEED you ask?

VOICE: Don't push me too. . . .

BERT: It's just that I'm so excited! Here's the first part of my plan: I'm not going to say a word!

VOICE: Well, thank . . . ME, for that!

BERT: I'll just BE and DO! And then, when people come and ask WHY or WHAT I am and do . . . then, and only then, shall I speak! And I shall speak little more than these words: what I am is what I AM is!

VOICE: Might I suggest. . . .

BERT: You're right, it IS a very simple statement . . . BUT . . . it is a profound statement! LEAN AND STRONG! Like me . . . like I! Remember, I don't want to become preachy . . . or wordy . . . or mouthy . . . the type that yaks and yaks and yaks on and on and on and on. . . .

VOICE: WHEN?

BERT: When?

VOICE: When will you BEGIN exercising the godly practice of . . . silence?

BERT: Right now!

VOICE: Good. Then I can say goodbye.

BERT: But you'll come when I call?

VOICE: No.

BERT: NO? ? ? You're DESERTING ME!

VOICE: Of course not! I will come to you when *I* choose to come!

BERT: Since I'm now practicing silence . . . I can't ask WHY? ? ? ?

VOICE: I have learned that a Christian would have me so ever-present that he ceases to be a man!

BERT: Would you repeat that?

VOICE: No.

BERT: But what does it mean?

VOICE: What does "I am what I AM is" mean? ? ?

BERT: I don't know for sure . . . but I'm working on it!

VOICE: You do that. And now. . . .

BERT: Goodbye . . . friend? ?

VOICE: Goodbye . . . friend!

[BERT *remains silent for a moment; then telephone rings; he answers it.*]

BERT: Hello.

MOTHER: Ethelbert? This is your mother.

BERT: Yes, mother?

MOTHER: You're alone now?

BERT: I'm alone.

MOTHER: What did Leon say about Portnoy?

BERT [*pause*]: Nothing.

MOTHER: I don't blame him! It's too filthy to talk about!

BERT: Mother?

MOTHER: Yes?

BERT: From now on. . . .

MOTHER: Yes?

BERT: Call me . . . Bert.

[*He hangs up.*]   (END)

37

Do You Mean to Say that Manure Is the Only Answer?

A chancel drama of sorts based upon a rather free reading of Luke 13:6–9

Characters

TOM: Thirtyish and large; Executive Secretary, Bureau of Statistics, Schwartz, Schwartz, and Schwartz Vineyards, Ltd.; he aspires to become director of the bureau (N.B. it's a one-man bureau).

JERRY: Thirtyish and small; Assistant to the Director, Records Division, Schwartz, Schwartz, and Schwartz Vineyards, Ltd.; he aspires to become associate director of the division (N.B. it's a one-man division).

REUBEN: Late-teenish; each cautious step he makes toward adulthood is followed by two sure leaps back into adolescence; but he will mature markedly under pressure.

REBECCA: Mid-teenish and beautiful; Schwartz's beloved daughter; Reuben's beloved; she's already accepted him in spite of his unacceptability; their marriage will survive, even triumph.

SCHWARTZ: Fiftyish; President of the Company; Chairman of the Board; a demanding but good boss; a concerned but understanding daddy; Rebecca is lucky; Reuben, luckier.

BRUNO: Twentyish; quite small but compensatorally spunky; Pruner Extraordinaire, Schwartz, Schwartz, and Schwartz Vineyards, Ltd.; a college drop-out, he now yearns to return to academia to do his cutting down; he's definitely Ph.D. material.

TREE: Alive and kicking.

Time

The first third of the first century, that point in history that is both dated and dateless, depending on whether you are looking at a calendar or in a mirror.

Setting

A part of the vineyard.

40

Do You Mean to Say
that Manure Is the Only Answer?

[TOM *and* JERRY *enter; they are taking inventory; each tree is numbered (four of the trees can be made in a variety of ways: posters, actual models, etc.; the fig tree is a costumed actor);* TOM *calls out number and type,* JERRY *checks them against numbers in book he's carrying; it's been a long, hot day; both men are tired.*]

TOM: Tree number 136. . . .

JERRY [*writing in book*]: Tree number 136. . . .

TOM: Orange tree!

JERRY: Orange tree.

TOM: Tree number 137. . . .

JERRY: Tree number 137. . . .

TOM: Apple tree!

JERRY: Apple tree.

TOM: Tree number 138. . . .

JERRY: Tree number 138. . . .

TOM: Banana tree!

JERRY: Banana tree.

TOM: Tree number 139. . . .

JERRY: Tree number 139. . . .

Tom: Christmas tree!

Jerry: Christmas tree.

Tom: Tree number 140. . . .

Jerry: Tree number 140. . . .

Tom: Wait a minute. . . .

Jerry: Wait a minute. . . .

Tom: Well, I'll be damned!

Jerry: You most certainly will if you continue to use language like that!

Tom: Isn't tree number 140 registered as a fig tree?

Jerry [*turning to back-section of notebook*]: Tree number 140 . . . yes, yes . . . it is a fig tree.

Tom: It is NOT a fig tree!

Jerry: It is ! !

Tom: NOT ! ! No figs ! !

Jerry: Well, I'll be damned! I mean . . . I'll be DARNED!

Tom: Tree number 140 is definitely NOT a fig tree!

Jerry: You're joking.

Tom: Joking, sir? About FIG trees? Perhaps about the occasional kumquat bush . . . but a fig tree? Never!

JERRY: Then this is NOT a fig tree??? Let's hope that this is only a clerical error and not a botanical . . . ABERRATION!

TOM: Well, we've got some kind of a booboo here but I think we can settle it p.d.q.!

JERRY: I'm afraid that I don't share your optimism! The flying, fickle, finger of fate has flung us face-first before a figless fig tree! Fie, fie, fie! What are we going to do?

TOM: No problem . . . just take your pencil and ERASE the word FIG.

JERRY: I can't!

TOM: Then just cross it out!

JERRY: I WON'T!

TOM: Come on, man . . . look at it this way: we've got no figs so we've got no fig tree! But . . . we've got a trunk, branches, leaves, and shade! So we've at least got us a tree! And it's enough to be a tree!

JERRY: Sentimental drivel! Scientific hog-wash! Economic ruination! A tree is not JUST a tree! You may think it is, I may think it is . . . BUT . . . the Big Boss doesn't think it is! He's a both-and'er! Both tree AND fruit! Tree as tree simply doesn't exist!

TOM: But there it is! A fact! You do believe in the

scientific world-view, don't you! There is a tree: figless but alive!

JERRY: And YOU believe in the prophetic world-view, don't you! There is a tree . . . figless and . . . DEAD! Come on, we must report this. [*Exits.*]

TOM [*trying to comfort the tree*]: Well, look at it this way: one man's figless fig tree is another man's . . . kindling! [*Exits.*]
[REUBEN *enters; checks to see that no one else is around; moves to the "tree" and speaks grandly.*]

REUBEN: Noble tree! [*He bows and the tree returns the bow.*] Oh, thou silent witness to our love, I salute thee! [*He salutes and the tree returns the salute.*] At least I hope to heaven that you are a SILENT witness! [*A red spot light shines on the tree; the tree blushes.*] If I thought for one moment that you were a blabber mouth, I'd . . . I'd . . . I'd kick the pith out of you! [*The tree shakes in fear.*] Ah, Rebecca . . . my sweet Rebecca! [*He turns deliriously.*] My soft-sweet-lovely-fragrant-beauteous Rebecca! [*He wanders silently for a moment, lost in sweet anticipation.*] I know what I'll do! I'll compose a verse with which to welcome her to today's tryst. Let me see . . . [*He cogitates.*] . . . no, I think I read that somewhere . . . let me see . . . no, that's too insipid. . . . I want something fresh . . . something daringly original. . . . [*Suddenly*] I've got it!

Search the heavens
Where the angel cavorts
And you'll find none sweeter
Than Rebecca Schwartz!

[*The tree holds its "nose."*] Ah, Rebecca! For you
I would . . . dive to the bottom of the Dead Sea!
I would . . . would . . . turn the Red Sea puce!
[*Turning quickly and addressing the tree*] But if
she's not here by the time I count to one hundred
I'm going home! [*As he starts counting out loud,
Rebecca tiptoes in behind him; she watches with
amusement; when he gets to eight she gives a loud
BOO!*] What in the hel . . . lo, my beloved! [*They
embrace.*]

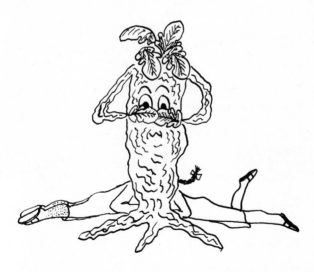

45

REBECCA [*teasingly*]: Did your heart jump a little?

REUBEN: No, but my bladder quivered a bit!

[*He sits under tree 140 and she sits beside him; he then stretches out and places his head in her lap; the top of the tree bends over as if to watch the proceedings.*]

REBECCA: What were you counting, my love?

REUBEN [*stalling*]: I . . . I wasn't counting anything.

[*He tries to kiss her.*]

REBECCA: Yes you were. Now tell me . . . what were you counting?

REUBEN: O.K. I was counting. . . .

REBECCA: What?

REUBEN: Nothing . . . just nothing.

[*He tries to kiss her again; she'll not be sidetracked.*]

REBECCA: The clouds in the sky? Blades of grass? The leaves on this tree!

REUBEN: No, my sweet. . . . I was counting your . . . qualities!

REBECCA [*lightly*]: Really? And you could think of only eight?

REUBEN [*not sure that he's off the hook yet*]: Oh, no . . . not at all! I was just beginning to count . . .

why, I would have reached . . . a million if you hadn't come!

REBECCA: And which of my qualities had you counted?

REUBEN: I began with your beauty [*he tries to kiss her*] . . . your intelligence . . . [*she laughs lightly and pushes his head away*] . . . your wit . . . your charm, your charity, your chastity, your . . .

[*Chastity was the wrong word; she speaks very abruptly.*]

REBECCA: MY WHAT? ? ?

REUBEN: Your chasti. . . .

[*Before he can repeat the word she is standing up; angry and hurt.*]

REBECCA: Reuben Bloomberg you are a cruel person! You're mean . . . and callous . . . and . . . what's worse . . . FORGETFUL! [*She begins to weep.*] How could you? How could you . . . forget?

REUBEN [*still on the ground*]: But I didn't! I haven't forgotten . . . and I won't forget!

REBECCA [*walking to another tree*]: Yes you did . . . you have . . . and you will!

REUBEN [*standing up and walking toward her*]: Now, now, now . . . I HAVEN'T forgotten! Why, it seems like it was just last month!

REBECCA [*fiercely*]: It WAS last month! [*walking away from him*] And you've already forgotten!

REUBEN: Listen to me. . . . I haven't forgotten! Man alive, I haven't forgotten! When I was running through that list . . . I was just using a little . . . poetic license. It just seemed so natural to move from charm to charity to . . . [*gulping*] chastity.

REBECCA: Well, last month you must have been using plenty of poetic LIBERTY to move from . . . hugging . . . to kissing . . . to . . . well, you know what! And you said . . . [*much weeping*] . . . and you said that they were all parts of the same . . . DYNAMIC!

REUBEN: They are, my darling, they are! And didn't I also say . . . come on, now, listen to me . . . didn't I also say that we were now QUASI-OFFICIALLY married? Answer me . . . didn't I say that? We are now married! I did say that didn't I?

REBECCA: Oh, yes, you said that. You told me [*quick sobs*] and . . . and you told God . . . [*more sobs*] . . . but when are you going to tell my FATHER?

REUBEN [*gulping*]: Your father. . . .

REBECCA: My father.

REUBEN: Your father . . . well . . . of course I am going to tell him. . . . I am DEFINITELY going to tell him . . . but. . . .

REBECCA [*she is no longer weeping*]: But? ? ?

REUBEN: Well . . . your father is so . . . so. . . .

REBECCA: Yes? ? ?

REUBEN: Your father is so . . . AWESOME!

REBECCA [*with rising anger*]: Oh Reuben . . . you're beautiful . . . I mean you are REALLY beautiful!

REUBEN [*he responds quietly*]: Thank you.

REBECCA: If you are so . . . speechless . . . so voiceless . . . so DUMB when confronted by awesomeness . . . then how in the world did you dare tell GOD we were married!

REUBEN: That's a good question, Rebecca. It shows real insight. But the fact of the matter is . . . well, it's just that your father's awesomeness is more . . . immediate!

REBECCA: What you mean is that he might break your neck now rather than waiting for the sweet justice of eternity!

REUBEN [*with unexpected candor*]: You are so RIGHT! No . . . that's not it! Now don't worry. I am going to tell him! I'm just waiting, watching, planning for the propitious moment! And then. . . .

REBECCA: Reuben.

REUBEN: . . . and then I'm going to. . . .

REBECCA: Reuben!

REUBEN: Yes?

REBECCA: The moment is more propitious than you think!

REUBEN [*pauses; speaks cautiously*]: PRESSINGLY propitious?

REBECCA [*rolling the 'r'*]: Pressingly.

REUBEN [*with widening eyes*]: You're kidding?

REBECCA: No . . . and . . . Yes!

REUBEN [*he picks her up and twirls her about*]: Oh, Rebecca, my darling! This is wonderful! How marvelous! How terrific! I feel like shouting the news to highest heaven!

REBECCA: Heaven already knows, my sweet! DADDY doesn't!

REUBEN [*with new-found boldness*]: Well, I'm going to tell him right now! [*Pauses*] No, I'll wait until after supper . . . no . . . first thing in the morning . . . first thing in the morning I'll tell him . . . right after lunch.

REBECCA: If I were listing your qualities guess how far down the list COURAGE would be?

REUBEN: This is not a question of courage! It's really . . . well, it's really a question of wisdom. And I'm

50

just a little bit hurt that you don't trust me. I had hoped that you would have seen that what I'm waiting for is the right occasion . . . and the right words! [*Suddenly; he's got it.*] I've got it! I've got it! I'll walk right up to him, place my hands firmly on his shoulders, look him straight in the eye and say, "Mr. Schwartz! I've got good news for you, great news for you! Your daughter is definitely NOT barren!" What do you think of that? I mean . . . there's nothing that a vineyard owner is more terrified of than barrenness!

REBECCA: Maybe it's because I'm just a simple, little country girl . . . unschooled in the inner logic of sophisticated persuasive techniques . . . but my womanly intuition tells me that it is quite unlikely that your words will move my father to kill the fatted calf! About the best you could expect is a cooked goose!

REUBEN [*asks the tree*]: What do you think? [*Tree nods in agreement.*] Hmmmmm . . . well, O.K! I agree . . . that was pretty bad. Then I'll do it this way. [*Playacting*] Mr. Schwartz, sir! Life is filled with surprises! It may surprise you to know that for years now you've been a second father to me. It may surprise you even more to know that for the past month or so you've been a father-in-law to me! Shake, dad! [*Turning enthusiastically to* REBECCA] What'd you think of that?

REBECCA: Well, at least it's a little less CLINICAL! But I'm not sure . . . folksy as it is . . . I'm not sure that it would make father embrace you rather than STRANGLE you!

REUBEN: Goodness, Rebecca, you make your father sound so . . . physical!

REBECCA: Aren't ALL men . . . in one way or another? It's just a matter of which muscle they . . . flex!

REUBEN: Honey, your insightfulness overwhelms me! It also gives me a great idea! Why don't YOU tell your father the . . . good news?

REBECCA [dumbfounded]: Reuben? ? ? ? ?

REUBEN: All right . . . all right! I was just fooling. Come on, let's go.

REBECCA: Where?

REUBEN: We're going to see your father right now!

REBECCA: But what are you going to say?

REUBEN: Don't worry . . . I'll think of something. Maybe my forte is really simple, spontaneous honesty!

REBECCA: I don't know . . . I'm afraid. . . .

REUBEN: Of HONESTY????

REBECCA: In the hands of the inexperienced, yes!

REUBEN: Gee, Becky . . . you sure know how to hurt a guy!

[*From off stage we hear* JERRY *shout: "Right this way, Mr. Schwartz! And I hope you aren't too shocked by what you see!"*]

REBECCA [*running to* REUBEN]: My father! What are we going to do? Do you want to talk to him HERE?

[*Off stage* TOM *says: "There's no need to hurry, Mr. Schwartz! It's a pretty sorry sight!"*]

REUBEN: Let's think about it . . . behind that rock! [*He drags her behind a big rock.*]

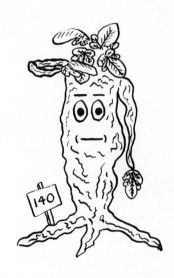

Tom [*enters first*]: Here it is! Tree 140.

Jerry [*enters with* Schwartz]: It's true, it's absolutely true, it's tragically true . . . tree 140 . . . an alleged fig tree . . . is figless! You can search the ground, scrutinize the branches, and you'll find no fig!

[*Tree begins to shake mildly.*]

Tom: Right, boss! We've been real scientific about the whole thing . . . checked this and that . . . rechecked facts and figures . . . verified the whole business. This tree is a fraud!

[*Tree shakes with growing violence.*]

Schwartz [*he's not been listening to the men; his trained eye has been on the tree; after a brief moment he speaks rather solemnly*]: Cut it down!

[*The tree "faints."*]

Tom: Yes, sir! Gladly, sir! Just as soon as Bruno gets here with the ax. [*Yelling off stage*] Get the lead out, Bruno!

Jerry: Hurry up man . . . and don't put any nicks on that blade! Oh boy, this is going to be fun! Goodbye, you ol' good-for-nothing tree!

Schwartz: Gentlemen! You don't seem to understand. We're cutting down a tree. This is no time for joy. It's a time for sorrow!

TOM [*rapid shift in mood*]: Oh, I know it, boss! I really feel bad. Poor old tree!

JERRY [*similarly*]: Yes . . . [*walks up to tree and pats it*] it's going to hurt me worse than it does you!

[*The tree revives enough to shake its head.*]

[BRUNO *enters; he is wearing the traditional executioner's outfit including black mask; he is carrying, with great difficulty, a huge ax; he staggers over to the tree and slowly, with great difficulty, gets the ax off his shoulder; he tries to lean it against the tree; the tree knocks it down; this is repeated three times; finally* BRUNO *just leaves it on the ground; he wipes his brow and breathes deeply.*]

BRUNO: What a way to make a living! Many are the times I wish that I had finished college. Oops . . . excuse me. [*He turns his back to the audience/congregation and "fixes" something.*] My truss slipped! I don't face too many occupational hazards but the ones I do are terribly . . . personal. [*Pointing to tree 140.*] That's the victim?

TOM: Right!

BRUNO: This is the hour?

JERRY: Righto! [*Checks his jubilation when he remembers* SCHWARTZ'S *words.*] Alas, 'tis so.

BRUNO [*looking around*]: So where is the drum corps?

Tom: The what?

Bruno: The drum corps. Union regulations require that I be provided a sharp ax and a snappy drum corps!

Jerry: But this isn't your usual kind of execution. It's more like . . . corrective surgery.

Bruno: Yeh? Well you just try telling that tree that it'll be happier as a stump!

Schwartz [*solemnly*]: This IS an execution. The evidence has been gathered. The verdict given. The sentence is just.

[Tom *and* Jerry *snap to attention and pretend they are a drum corps: ratatattating etc.*]

Bruno: Now I KNOW I should have finished college!

[*He takes a strip of black cloth from his pocket and ties it around the trunk at eye-level; he begins to offer it a cigarette; then he spits on his hands and begins a very laborious effort of getting the ax to his shoulder; the men are ratatattating; the tree is quivering; just when he has the ax precariously poised for the blow,* Reuben *and* Rebecca, *who have watched the entire proceedings from behind the rock, jump out shouting "No, don't do it! Stop him . . . stop him . . . etc.";* Bruno *is startled, drops the ax or rather is pulled over backwards by it;* Rebecca *runs to her father;* Reuben *jumps on* Bruno.]

REBECCA: Oh, father, please don't let him cut it down! He mustn't . . . he simply mustn't!

[TOM and JERRY *pull* REUBEN *off* BRUNO.]

REUBEN [*still held by the two*]: Fath . . . Mr. Schwartz, sir! This tree has great sentimental value for Rebecca and me! In the name of your forefathers, your children, and your children's children, in the name of humanity do not let him cut down this noble tree!

REBECCA: Please listen to him, father!

[SCHWARTZ *nods to the two men who release* REUBEN; BRUNO *has been sitting on the ground but he now gets up and brushes himself off.*]

BRUNO: This is one occcupational hazard I hadn't counted on! Wait'll the union hears about this! [*He turns and fixes his truss again.*]

SCHWARTZ [*directly but not harshly*]: Just what is it you have to say, young man?

REUBEN: Thank you, sir. Now if I may just gather my thoughts for a minute . . . I'm not a violent person . . . no, I should say not . . . I'm all for passive resistance . . . and that sort of stuff. I'm not sure how I should put this . . . maybe this way [*he strikes a rather classic pose*]:
   Woodsman, spare that tree!
   Touch not a single bough

57

In my youth it sheltered me
And I'll protect it now!

SCHWARTZ: I'm afraid you'll have to do better than that!

REUBEN [*thinking under pressure*]: Very good, sir . . . yes . . . now let me see . . . how about this?

I think that I shall never see,
A poem lovely as a tree.
A tree that looks at God all day
And lifts her leafy arms to pray!

[*The tree brings two branches together as if folding hands.*]

SCHWARTZ: Why don't you try prose . . . original prose, if you don't mind.

REUBEN: O.K. . . . O.K. . . . if that's your wish . . . I'll try.

REBECCA [*runs to him*]: And you'll succeed . . . I know you'll succeed! Search yourself . . . look deeply . . . and you'll find a vast reservoir of hithertofore UNUSED wisdom, valor, and common sense. Reuben, I'm counting on you to save this tree, our tree!

BRUNO: If he pulls this off, missy, it'll mean that the age of miracles is still with us which means that I'll go back to college as an adult special!

REUBEN [*much impressed with his new role as defender of the lost*]: Mr. Schwartz! [*His voice soars too high and cracks a bit; he readjusts it.*] Mr. Schwartz, sir! Your honor . . . your eminence . . . your worship! Our defense of this tree is based on the very substructure of creation itself, viz. [*he pronounces "viz"*] LOVE! Since this is a manifestly self-evident truth we shall not attempt to prove it . . . we simply PROCLAIM it! This means that not just this tree but indeed humanity itself is on trial! Today arborcide! Tomorrow genocide!!

BRUNO: You can tell he's a college man!

REUBEN [*playing to an imagined jury*]: We will show . . . we will RESPECTFULLY show that the evidence on which this hapless harbinger of heaven's handiwork stands convicted is flimsy, circumstantial, myopic and . . . and . . . and not very nice!

REBECCA [*bringing him back to reality*]: Reuben . . . it was my father who evaluated and APPROVED the evidence!

REUBEN [*right in step*]: On the other hand, a powerfully good case can be made for the unassailability of the evidence! Therefore we propose to . . . to throw ourselves on the mercy of the court! In so doing, we wish to remind you of the immortal words of Rabbi ben-Apriori, viz. [*pronounced*]: The quantity of mercy is not sifted!

JERRY [*wanting a piece of the action*]: Your honor, may I speak a word in support of the prosecution? [SCHWARTZ *nods affirmatively.*] Thank you, your worship! [*He struts around for a moment.*] The first thing that the prosecution wishes to say is that we willingly support the proposition that Justice is impartial hence, as they say, blind! but we just as willingly contest the defense's apparent presupposition that justice is sentimental hence stupid!

TOM: 'Ats right, your honor! [*Adding with dramatic flourish*] Down with STUPIDITY! [SCHWARTZ *gives him a withering look;* TOM *had been sitting down—standing only for the last line—he now sits down.*]

JERRY: May I apologize to the court for my colleague's . . . exuberance. Now, if I may, I would like to return to the heart of the matter and in so doing remind the defense that the issue is starkly simple. I might add that this is one of the few times in my long legal career when I can say, unequivocally, that justice CAN be determined by direct yes's and no's! [TOM *will join him on the yes's and no's.*] Is the defendent a fig tree? YES! Is the raison-d'etre—how do you say in English?—is the JUSTIFICATION for the tree's existence rooted in the production of figs? YES! In the absence of figs is such justification lost? YES! Without justification is there any hope for life? NO! Does this fig tree have any figs? NO!

Should it be cut down? YES! [*Assuming he has disemboweled* REUBEN, *he whips the following off quickly.*] Your witness!

REUBEN: Facts, facts, facts . . . as though they were the STUFF of justice! Furthermore, the defense objects to the conclusion that sentiment is the blood enemy of pure reason . . . as though the feelings that one may have about something or someone are void of rational . . . ah . . . substantive . . . ah . . . ah . . . OR one could put it this way . . . ah . . . we would argue that there are historically veri- fiable reasons why one feels the way he feels about something or someone . . . ah . . . which is just another way of saying that . . . that. . . .

REBECCA [*knowing that he is way over his head*]: Psst! Reuben! [*He comes to her and she whispers in his ear; his face lights up; he quickly goes to* JERRY *for an eyeball-to-eyeball encounter.*]

REUBEN: O.K., Mr. Yes and No Man . . . there is one question . . . one very IMPORTANT question you DIDN'T ask! Answer me this . . . yes or no . . . did you ever once ask WHY the tree is figless? Did you ask that question? No, you didn't ask that question? Why don't you answer? Not important you say! Not important? Not important? [*Forgets next line; whispers audibly to* REBECCA.] Why is it important again?

REBECCA [*disgusted*]: Honestly, Reuben . . . I . . .

REUBEN [*remembering*]: Why is it important, you ask? I'll tell why: it's the only truly HUMAN question! That's why. Even the lower animals can ask: who, what, where, when, and how! Only a man can ask WHY?

TOM [*puzzled*]: My dog doesn't ask me none of those questions! He justs barks, bites, snarls, and scratches.

REUBEN: If you weren't so dumb you'd know that there was a who, what, where, when, and how coming from each one of those activities! [*Turning back to* JERRY] Did you ask the question? Yes or No? NO! Why not? Your witness, BUSTER!

BRUNO [*he's been examining the tree, particularly the trunk, during the preceding proceedings*]: Just a little minute, friends and neighbors. I think I've solved the mystery. I think I know why this tree is barren!

[REUBEN *and* REBECCA *are excited; they ask, "You do? Really? Did you hear that? How wonderful! This is great!" etc.*]

JERRY: Your honor, I object to this lame attempt to introduce scurrilous evidence into these proceedings! This is nothing more than the mealy-mouthed machinations of a hatchet man gone soft!

SCHWARTZ: Objection overruled. You may proceed.

BRUNO: Thank you, your eminence. May it please the

court to know that someone has been carving up a storm on the backside of this trunk! With the court's permission I shall try to decipher those carvings! Then we'll know the REAL culprits!

SCHWARTZ: Proceed.

BRUNO [*taking a pair of granny glasses from his pocket, he breathes on them and cleans them with the blindfold he's taken from around the tree; he gets on his hands and knees, rubs the trunk clearing away dust, etc., squints and speaks slowly*]: The first carving . . . it looks like the oldest . . . is a kind of crudely made little heart with the letters . . . R and . . . R in it. [REUBEN *and* REBECCA *look at each other and begin to slink to the side of the*

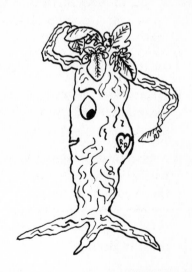

stage/chancel.] Just a little bit higher is a larger heart . . . entwined with another heart with the words . . . Rebecca and Reuben in them. [*Everyone looks at the guilty couple.*] Then up here is a . . . yes, it's a sentence . . . that reads: Reuben likes . . . no . . . there's a hash mark through likes and above it is the word . . . l-o-v-e-s . . . yes, that's it: Reuben loves Rebecca. [*He's getting quite excited.*] And here at the top is a kind of long sentence . . . oh, great scott . . . listen to THIS! Reubie Pie Kissed His Becky Wecky By This Tree Under a Full September Moon . . . and then there's a . . . a date, I guess! [*He turns good naturedly to* REUBEN.] Reuben, my boy . . . you're a pretty fine man with a knife! Have you ever thought of moving up . . . say to an AX? Anyway, may it please the court to know that it is my professional judgment that these carvings have made this tree figless!

TOM [*contemptuously*]: Butchers!

REBECCA [*runs to her father*]: Oh, daddy, we didn't mean any harm! Surely those . . . silly little things couldn't have been that damaging!

REUBEN: Becky's right! Why . . . the little penknife I used couldn't have made it even half-way through the bark! And anyway . . . I don't believe that cosmic justice would let any expression of true love . . . however it's expressed . . . be an instrument of death!

64

JERRY [*delighted that they have won the point for him*]: I couldn't have put it more convincingly myself! [*Contemptuously to* BRUNO] Since even . . . CHILDREN . . . can refute your self-proclaimed expertise, I trust that you will now refrain from further interruptions!

REBECCA [*running to* REUBEN]: What have we done . . . what have we done?

REUBEN: It's all right, honey! We haven't lost yet!

JERRY: Ah tenacity! Sweet, sweet tenacity! In the hands of adolescents it becomes that doglike quality of confusing wishbone for backbone.

[REUBEN *angrily runs over and picks up* BRUNO'S *ax; as he chases* JERRY *around the stage/chancel,* REBECCA *shrieks and goes to* BRUNO; TOM *tries to hide behind a tree;* JERRY *finally crouches down behind* SCHWARTZ; SCHWARTZ *steps away from* JERRY *who doesn't realize that he is now exposed in a posture that invites decapitation;* REUBEN *lifts the ax, then rather than using it, drops it and very matter of factly resumes the questioning, bending over to direct his words to a still quivering* JERRY.]

REUBEN: Oh, yeh??? And here's another question you haven't answered . . . haven't even considered for that matter! What could be done to get this tree producing again? Did you ever ask THAT question? NO, you didn't! Why not??

JERRY [*stands up, brushes himself off and continues as though nothing had happened*]: Because it's an irrelevant question! It's not . . . germane!

REUBEN: I'll tell you why you haven't asked that question! It's because . . . well . . . you really aren't interested in figs . . . you're not even interested in LIFE! You're just interested in DEATH!

TOM [*intrigued*]: He did kick my dog once!

JERRY [*grandly*]: I'm interested in JUSTICE!

REUBEN: In your rumpeled little mind, sir, justice and death mean the same thing!

JERRY [*appealing to* SCHWARTZ]: Your reverence, in all my years before the bar I've never, NEVER been subjected to such . . . such . . . un-niceness! I trust that your worship will charge him with contempt of court! [SCHWARTZ *says nothing;* JERRY *waits self-righteously; when* SCHWARTZ *remains silent,* JERRY *adds nervously*] Or . . . should we incarcerate him this very minute?

BRUNO: Not with MY ax you won't!

SCHWARTZ [*quietly to* REUBEN]: I have a hunch that, given your emotional attachment to this particular tree, you really aren't interested in the fig question either. If he is just interested in the DEATH of the tree . . . period . . . isn't it just as likely that

you are interested in the LIFE of the tree . . .
period?

REUBEN: Yes, sir! I mean . . . when this trial began
I WAS just interested in saving this tree! The court
doesn't realize just how much this tree means to
Becky and me. We've spent some wonderful moments here! [*Red spot shines on the tree for a moment.*] And just as soon as these proceedings are
over I intend to tell you, your honor. But NOW I
am really interested in the fig question. You can
trust me, sir! Honesty is one of my greatest . . .
[*he looks at* REBECCA, *gulps, and sort of squeaks
out the following word*] aspirations. [*Regaining his
composure.*] Now, if I may, I would like to return
to the case and pursue a line of questioning that
may not APPEAR to be of immediate relevance but
will, I trust, move us quickly to the heart of the
matter . . . to the heart of justice! May I proceed?

JERRY: Objection!

SCHWARTZ: Objection overruled!

JERRY: Overruled????

SCHWARTZ [*calmly*]: Overruled.

BRUNO [*patting his ax so that* JERRY *gets the point*]:
Overruled.

REUBEN: Thank you, your worship! Now . . . if I
may, I would like to request the assistance of the

prosecution in pursuing this new line of questioning.

JERRY: Ridiculous! Absurd! Unheard of! Impossible!
[BRUNO *has been running his finger along the edge
of the blade; he pretends to cut his finger, yells
"Ouch!"; looks threateningly to* JERRY, *who gulps
and continues.*] But . . . intriguing! And since I've
always had a soft spot in my heart for intrigue, how
may I help you?

REUBEN: Let's pretend for a moment. Let's pretend
that you are a man of faith.

JERRY: Sir . . . I resent that! I AM a man of faith!

REUBEN: But I'm thinking of a particular faith! Let's
pretend that you are one of the Carpenter's Crew!

JERRY: The Carpenter's Crew??? You mean that tiny,
little SECT that's been making all kinds of whoop-
tidoo for the last couple of years?

REUBEN: That's right.

JERRY: You mean that you want me to pretend that
I'm one of those guys who say that they've left
everything to follow the Carpenter?

REUBEN: That's right.

JERRY: You want me to pretend that I "turn the other
cheek" . . . "pray for my enemies" . . . "do good
to those who despitefully use me" . . .

REUBEN: . . . that's right . . .

JERRY: . . . "who sell all that they have and give it to the poor" . . . "who love their neighbor as they do themselves" . . .

REUBEN: . . . that's right . . .

JERRY: . . . you want me to pretend that I believe that the Carpenter is God Himself . . . the Hope and Promise of everything and everyone?

REUBEN: That's right!

JERRY: I won't do it!

REUBEN: What do you mean . . . you won't do it?

JERRY: I just won't do it!

REUBEN: Why not?

JERRY: Man, that's a pretty wild scene! I mean . . . even PRETENDING to believe all those things . . . and do all that stuff could get to a guy after a while! I mean . . . I think it's too spooky to play around with!

REUBEN: Nonsense, my good fellows! Pretending to be one of the Carpenter's Crew is the easiest thing in the world! Hundreds of people are playing the game now and . . . who knows . . . some day millions will be playing it.

JERRY: I still have some grave reservations about

69

pretending to be one of the Carpenter's Crew. As I understand it . . . now please don't get me wrong . . . I do NOT mix with that kind of riff-raff . . . not at all, not at all . . . nor do I entertain any of their radical theological notions . . . nosireesir . . . the old time religion is good enough for me! ! ! What I know of them is completely secondhand . . . COMPLETELY secondhand! ! ! But, anyway, it is my understanding that they are very much concerned with lofty, noble, elevating issues. I mean, what could be loftier than getting all wrapped up in the question: COULD GOD BECOME MAN? ? ? Now, there's a question for you! ! It makes you want to lift your head . . . toward heaven! Swooshed up to the clouds . . . away from the hard-core, nitty-gritty facts of life! ! ! It all sounds so . . . HEAVENLY!

REUBEN: Ah, my friend, you'd better recheck your secondary sources! The Crew is not SUPPOSED to be wrapped up in the QUESTION: COULD GOD BECOME MAN! ! !

BRUNO: Ohhhhh . . . I don't know how much more of this I can stand! I simply must get my B.A.! Then I could REALLY appreciate the brilliance of this debate! ! As things stand now . . . it sounds pretty dumb!

JERRY: Not even a Ph.D. would help you!

BRUNO: But it might help the debate!

JERRY: You were saying?

REUBEN: The Crew is NOT wrapped up in a QUES-TION! Rather, they are committed to an AN-SWER! [*He has been gesturing vigorously.*]

BRUNO: I think I'll major in Religious Studies! I always was pretty good at gesturing! ! [*He tries a few.*]

REUBEN: Now, the interesting thing is that the AN-SWER, viz. [*pronounced*] the Carpenter, has ordered the Crew into the nitty-gritty, hard-core facts of life!

JERRY: What does that mean?

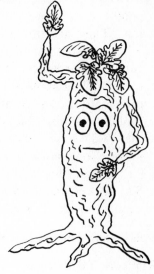

BRUNO [*with a grand gesture*]: Goodbye clouds . . . hello gutters! !

REUBEN [*delighted*]: That's right! That's right! That's absolutely right! !

BRUNO [*rapturously*]: So ordain me . . . ordain me . . . somebody ordain me! [*Tree does.*]

REUBEN: Now . . . let's move closer to the heart of the matter. The Carpenter has told the Crew that he expects a certain style of life from them . . . a style that is at least partially described by the things you mentioned earlier. BUT . . . the Crew figures otherwise. They're still all wrapped up in the cloud-bit. They figure that their task is to get other people all wrapped up in the clouds . . . all shouting "The Carpenter is the YES to the Question!" That becomes the single criterion of faithfulness. But the Carpenter, the ANSWER, keeps asking them: "What about the gutters . . . what about the nitty-gritty . . . what about PEOPLE?" The Crew shouts "Clouds!" He shouts "People!" They love the YES! He wants them to love PEOPLE. To make a long story short . . . they aren't producing . . . at least they aren't producing what he expects. So . . . pretend that you're the Carpenter . . . what would you do to them?

JERRY: So . . . now I'm the Carpenter am I?

REUBEN: That's right.

JERRY: And I have to decide what to do with this . . . barren Crew?

REUBEN: That's right!

JERRY [*pointing an accusing finger at* BRUNO]: I bet that YOU think I'm going to say, "Chop 'em down, chop 'em down!" [BRUNO *offers him his ax.*] Why don't you just take that . . . thing . . . and . . . trim your toe nails? [BRUNO *thinks this is a good idea; he sits down, pulls off a shoe and reveals his big toe sticking through a hole; he begins trimming;* JERRY *returns to* REUBEN.] First of all I'd study the situation thoroughly. I'd ask myself WHY they weren't producing. . . .

BRUNO: I'll tell you why!

JERRY: . . . for the love of Pete . . . O.K. . . . O.K. . . . inflict us with your wisdom!

BRUNO [*still working on his toes*]: If you go the CLOUD-YES route, the worst thing that can happen to you—except in rare instances—is that you're called a BLOODY FOOL! But go the PEOPLE-LOVE route and there's the real possibility that you might GET bloody . . . maybe even killed! And most of us would rather live as present-tense fools than be remembered as past-tense martyrs!

JERRY [*amazed; he walks over and shakes* BRUNO's *hand*]: Well put . . . well put! Now that that question is answered I'd have to fight my own desire to get rid of the nonproducers p.d.q.! If they really didn't want to be a part of the Crew . . . fine! . . . I would respect a non-Crew category! BUT . . . what I wouldn't respect . . . wouldn't tolerate . . . is a pretend crew member!

BRUNO [*putting his shoe back on*]: Push that too rigorously and all you'll have left is CREW as a concept! And concepts don't feed the hungry or clothe the naked!

REUBEN [*jumping into the argument; very excited by* BRUNO's *insight*]: That's the point! That is THE point! Wouldn't you do everything you could . . . absolutely everything that you could . . . to get them producing?

BRUNO: Right you are! The medium is the produce!

REUBEN [*he will get so wrapped up in what he is saying that he'll finally be pleading with all of them*]: Wouldn't you give them one more chance! I mean REALLY give them another chance! Wouldn't you even want to live with them, eat and drink with them, pray with them [*building in intensity*], talk to them, plead with them . . . PREACH to them! [*He pauses for the briefest moment; there is a genuine EUREKA look on his face.*] That's it! That is IT! [*Dramatically*] Manure is the answer!

ALL: WHAT? ? ! !

BRUNO: What a facile mind! From sermonizing to fertilizing in a single breath! Wonder if there's an organic relationship between the two?

REUBEN [*to* SCHWARTZ]: Preaching may or may not get the Carpenter's Crew out of the clouds and into the streets—maybe it'll take something else, I don't know—but I believe that manure . . . lots of manure will get figs back on this tree! You're interested in figs . . . I'm interested in figs . . . we're ALL interested in figs! Will you give it a try? Will you wait one more year? The tree may not deserve to live, but the need for figs is so great that . . . well . . . will you give the tree . . . will you give *us* another chance?

SCHWARTZ [*he looks at the tree; he looks at them*]: It's worth a try. Yes, you can have your year!

[*Everyone is deliriously happy;* BECKY *throws her arms around* REUBEN; *the tree clasps two branches over its head in victory;* JERRY *shakes hands with* TOM; BRUNO *kicks his ax off stage/chancel.*]

REBECCA: You've done it! You've done it! I'm so happy . . . so terribly happy! Darling, you were wonderful!

BRUNO: The age of miracles IS still present! I'm returning to college! [*He exits saying: "amo, amas, amat, amamus, amatis, amant."*]

Tom: And we'll start hauling in the manure right away! Four, five, or six loads . . . whatever it takes!

[*Bottom part of trunk rolls down over tree's shoes; it holds its nose with one branch; the men exit.*]

Rebecca [*she takes one of* Schwartz's *arms; they begin to exit with* Reuben *a half step behind them*]: And, now, daddy, Reuben and I have something to tell you.

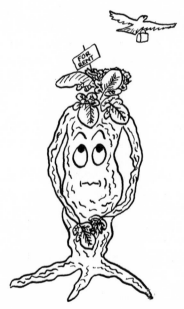

Reuben: That's right! And it is sort of concerned with production too!

[*They exit; after a second's time we hear* SCHWARTZ *bellow:* "YOU'RE WHAT? ? ? ?" *We hear* REUBEN *say joyfully:* "PUT IT THERE, DAD!" *Then* SCHWARTZ *says a very loud:* "OIVAY! !"]

(END)

Seventy Times Seven Equals Four-Hundred-Ninety But Then . . . POW!

A chancel drama of sorts based upon a rather free reading of Matthew 18:21

Characters

CAROL GURNEY PLOTTS: Thirtyish; Dexter's wife; at least they live together; she reflects the bloomlessness of their marriage; but she is capable of nearly instantaneous blossoming.

DEXTER Q. PLOTTS: Thirtyish; he's forgotten what it means to be a husband, but it is to his credit that he has had something to forget; his memory is just one step away from revival.

MOTHER: Fiftyish; a kind of carnivorous mother who, if the truth were known, longs to be herbivorous again.

Time

Today: that point in time that is brother to the regrets of the past and sister to the promises of the future.

Setting

The breakfast-dining room of the Plotts's New York apartment.

Seventy Times Seven Equals Four-Hundred-Ninety But Then . . . POW!

[*The action takes place in a combination kitchen-dining room; the only real pieces of furniture are a table and three chairs; stove, refrigerator, cupboards, etc. are all imagined; CAROL's actions in making the breakfast will be mimed; two portable chalkboards stand against the back wall; one is very nearly covered with hash-marks but the other is perfectly clear; CAROL is physically and emotionally done-in; her hair is messy; she hasn't as yet brushed her teeth so she occasionally smacks her lips, tongue, and teeth; she is wearing a faded chenille bathrobe that appears to be two sizes too large; she is lethargically preparing breakfast; after a moment or two her husband enters; he is well groomed and well dressed; he is wearing horn-rimmed eyeglasses; he is vain and spoiled; his actions are stuffy; he doesn't look at CAROL when he first enters; he stands looking into an imaginary mirror.*]

DEXTER: Showered . . . shaved . . . oh-so-sparingly scented. . . . [*pointing appropriately to his shoes, pants, shirt, and tie*] polished . . . pressed . . . lightly starched . . . topped off by the perfect windsor knot! [*Looking out of an imagined window, he says grandly*] Look out sunshine! Look out breezes! Look out morning! You've met your match! ! ! [*As he turns in his exuberance he sees his wife and nearly gags*] Well, you've done it again! Again, you've done it! Still, yet, and once more . . . you have done it! Done it! Done it! You have cast BLIGHT on this day's innocence . . . and on me! But . . . [*he reshapes the windsor knot, pulls at both shirt cuffs, removes his eyeglasses and tucks them in the breast-pocket of his suit coat; he then walks over to the heavily marked chalkboard, picks up a white glove lying on the chalk tray, takes a piece of chalk and makes another mark on the board; immediately after making the mark he turns to* CAROL *and says grandly*] I forgive you!

[*He puts down the piece of chalk, takes off the glove, puts on his eyeglasses, and appears to be a new man; he moves around the room with a kind of exuberance.*] Oh to be in New York . . . ALIVE . . . on a day like this! It makes me wish I were a poet! Now please do not misunderstand me! It's not that I'm ashamed of being an accountant . . . a CERTIFIED public accountant . . . but . . . this is the kind of a day that only a poet can drink to the dregs . . . metaphor-wise. But, as they say, it is better to be a half-sipper than a non-sipper . . . comparative-wise.

[*He looks around the room for a moment; half-laughingly, but barely concealing a barb, he speaks to his wife.*] You won't believe this . . . but I don't seem to see the morning paper. Isn't that funny?

[*As he continues searching, the barb becomes more*

82

obvious.] I don't see it on the coffee table, I don't see it on the book case, I don't see it on the otto-man, I don't see it on the sofa, I don't see it on my chair. . . . I JUST PLAIN DON'T SEE IT! [*He points an accusing finger at his wife.*] You . . . you didn't bring it in, did you? And don't tell me you forgot . . . or that you haven't had the time! I'll tell you why you didn't bring it in! You don't like me! You're trying to taunt me . . . to TEMPT me . . . to move me to ANGER! Well, let me tell you something! It won't work! Do you hear me? IT WON'T WORK! Because . . . [*he repeats the pre-vious action with eyeglasses, cuffs, glove, chalk, etc.*] I forgive you. [*He repeats the previous action of finishing with the chalk bit.*] I'll get it myself. [*He leaves and returns in a matter of seconds; pulling back one of the kitchen chairs, he sits down and begins to read the first section of the Sunday* Times.] This is unbelieveable . . . violence and more vio-lence! All over the world . . . violence and more violence. Murder . . . robbery . . . war . . . sabotage . . . rape . . . excuse me, ASSAULT . . . theft! And on and on it goes . . . and where it stops . . . nobody knows. The sun shines . . . the birds sing . . . the gentle rain falleth lightly . . . children laugh and jump . . . there are kittens and puppies . . . but still . . . violence . . . hatred . . . greed . . . selfishness . . . what's for breakfast, dear?

CAROL [*blandly*]: Eggs . . . easy-over.

83

DEXTER [*folding the paper on his lap in disgust*]: EASY-OVER?

CAROL: Scrambled?

DEXTER: SCRAMBLED? ?

CAROL: Soft boiled?

DEXTER: SOFT BOILED? ? ? Think, woman! This is SUNDAY! [*throwing the paper on the floor*]

CAROL: Eggs . . . sunny-side up.

DEXTER: I should hope so! [*He stands up and begins stalking around the room.*] For the love of Pete, I just can't understand you! How many years have we lived together . . . how many years have we been married? THREE!

CAROL: Only three?

DEXTER: How many Sunday breakfasts have we eaten? About ONE-HUNDRED-FIFTY! And now . . . you . . . you have the audacity to serve me eggs easy-over . . . on SUNDAY! Do you know what I could do . . . what I SHOULD do? Do you know what some husbands would do to THEIR wives if they did what you do . . . do you? Do you? But . . . [*he repeats the prior ritual*] I forgive you. [*He repeats the post ritual and returns to the chair and resumes reading the paper.*] I really must apologize. [CAROL *is surprised . . . shocked; she looks at him; he continues to read the paper as he speaks.*] I'm so

ashamed of my . . . ingratitude! My insensitivity is appalling! I am so hurtful! Downright cruel! I treat GOD so shabbily! [CAROL *does a double take and returns to cooking;* DEXTER, *without looking up, continues to read and to talk*.] With all of the starvation in the world . . . it is . . . unseemly that I should fly into a snit over a few eggs! I forget so easily that my cup runneth over and that my granary is gorged . . . metaphor-wise.
[CAROL *cracks an egg; the "sound" startles* DEXTER; *he places the paper on his lap*.] What was that?

CAROL: I cracked an egg.

DEXTER: You did what?

[*He throws the paper to the floor and stalks over to her*.]

CAROL [*not the least bit intimidated*]: An egg . . . I cracked it!

DEXTER: That's what I THOUGHT you said! How could you? How could you do such a thing? ? [CAROL *looks at him; she is amazingly patient*.] Mother's not here yet! What do you want her to do? Answer me! Do you want her to eat a COLD egg? Is that what you want her to do? I don't care how SUNNY the up-side is . . . if it's cold . . . even cool . . . gloom, gloom, GLOOM!

CAROL: You know I wouldn't serve a cold egg to . . . mumsie-pie.

85

DEXTER [*walking around the room*]: Oho! Now I see your plan! Make her eat Sunday breakfast by herself! Alone! ! That's it, isn't it? I eat now . . . and she eats later! I eat alone . . . she eats alone!

CAROL: I could eat with you.

DEXTER: Then mother would eat alone.

CAROL: So . . . I'll eat with her.

DEXTER: Then I'd eat alone!

CAROL: So I'll eat TWICE!

DEXTER: You're trying to come between me and

86

mother! That's what you're trying to do, isn't it? You have never loved her, right? You have never, never, never liked my mother, have you? Have you forgotten that I have lived with her longer . . . much, much longer than I've lived with you? And now you're trying to come between us. Do you know what I could do to you for such a heinous crime? Do you? Pretty terrifying, isn't it! HOW-EVER . . . [*he repeats the first part of the chalk-board bit*] I forgive you. [*He repeats the second part of the bit; just as he finishes,* MOTHER *walks in; she's dressed in her Sunday best; she walks directly to her son for her morning hug; she looks deceivingly motherly.*] Good morning, mother! Now the day is complete.

MOTHER: You are the sweet darling, aren't you?

DEXTER: Yes, mother.

CAROL: Good morning, Mother Plotts.

[MOTHER *looks at* CAROL, *then at* DEXTER, *and then back to* CAROL; *she begins to weep softly; her son comforts her.*]

DEXTER: There, there, mother . . . don't redden those beautiful eyes.

MOTHER: I'm all right, darling . . . it's just that in the morning . . . some parts of reality are just too . . . shocking . . . so drastically different from my DREAMS. But, don't fret. I'm all right now. [*She gives* DEXTER *another little kiss and, managing a strained smile, greets* CAROL.] Good morning, Carol Gurney.

CAROL [*nonvehemently*]: It's Plotts . . . Carol Gurney PLOTTS! I'm married to your son . . . remember?

[MOTHER *remembers and begins weeping again;* DEXTER *must comfort her once again; he speaks to his wife in a stage-whisper.*]

DEXTER: Must you be so brutally . . . direct? And so early in the morning?

CAROL [*replying in a stage-whisper*]: Would it be more comforting if I were your MISTRESS? [MOTHER, *with her face still buried in* DEXTER's *shoulder, shakes her head.*] How would it be if I were just your HOUSEKEEPER?

MOTHER [*turns from* DEXTER; *she is smiling broadly*]: Then my dreams would have come true!

DEXTER: Well, now, let's have breakfast.

[DEXTER *seats his mother and then sits down;* CAROL *remains standing waiting for him to seat her but he has already folded his hands and bowed his head.*]

Shall we offer thanks?

[MOTHER *immediately folds her hands and bows her head;* CAROL *is still standing; without changing from the posture of prayer, he whispers loudly to* CAROL.]

88

Where are your manners, Carol? We're going to pray!

[*She still stands; finally, though his head is still bowed,* DEXTER *reaches over with one hand and clumsily helps her with the chair; when she is seated, she folds her arms across her chest, bows her head and appears to fall asleep;* DEXTER *speaks at his stentorian best.*]

For the gifts we are about to receive, may we be truly grateful! And help us to be always mindful of the needs of others! Amen.

[MOTHER *repeats the "Amen"; she and* DEXTER *proceed to fluff their napkins and place them on their laps;* CAROL *remains in the posture of prayer or sleep; mother and son look at each other for a moment, then to* CAROL *and then back to each other; after he has cleared his throat loudly several times, and as the time is becoming awkwardly long, he whispers loudly.*]

Carol . . . Carol . . . [*he finally reaches over and touches her arm*] CAROL!

CAROL [*responding slowly*]: Yes?

MOTHER [*fanning herself with her napkin*]: Honestly, how anyone can fall asleep during morning prayers is beyond me! !

CAROL [*putting her elbows on the table and leaning her chin on her hands, she speaks rather slowly, reflectively*]: It wasn't that I was dozing, mumsie-dear.

89

MOTHER: Well, you APPEARED to be dozing!

CAROL [*nonvindictively*]: And you appeared to be praying. . . . But I was just thinking . . . thinking about "being mindful of the needs of OTHERS." [DEXTER *and* MOTHER *look at each other quizically; they remain silent as* CAROL *repeats the phrase with different inflections.*] MINDFUL of the needs of others . . . mindful of the NEEDS of others. . . .

MOTHER: What ARE you talking about?

CAROL: What we were PRAYING about. You do remember, don't you?

MOTHER [*she throws her napkin on her plate, gets up and walks peevishly from the table*]: I don't know how much more of this I can stand!

CAROL [*still nonvindictively*]: You've endured the past three years pretty well . . . and I'd guess you're good for another. . . .

MOTHER [*barking at* DEXTER]: Did you hear that? Did you hear that! She as good as told me to leave this house . . . to pack and leave . . . to leave my one and only son. . . . [*It appears that she is going to weep but after the first, light sniffle she turns warlike to* DEXTER.] Don't just sit there! DO something!

DEXTER: I don't DARE tell you what I'd LIKE to do! [*He pushes his chair back from the table.*] But I will tell you what I am GOING to do! I'm going to . . . [*He stands up and begins the eyeglasses/ chalkboard routine; but* MOTHER *will have none of this; she rushes to him and grabs him.*]

MOTHER: Oh, no you don't! ! [*To her great surprise,* DEXTER *struggles to get loose; she suddenly drops her arms to her side and says very loudly*] DEXTER! THIS IS MOTHER SPEAKING! FORGIVENESS HAS ITS TIME AND PLACE . . . BUT MOTHER HAS HERS TOO! ! !

DEXTER: But, mother! It's SUNDAY!

[*This announcement moves her; she sort of collapses on her chair at the breakfast table; she weeps softly and waves her napkin in assent.*]

MOTHER: All right . . . all right . . . that which you must do . . . do quickly!

[*He goes through the entire routine but doesn't say the magic words; he returns to the breakfast table and tries to get things back to normal.*]

DEXTER: Now, let's have breakfast.

CAROL [*she has been apparently oblivious to the exchange between* MOTHER *and* DEXTER*; she still has elbows on the table and chin in hands*]: No . . . let's talk THEOLOGY!

DEXTER [*flinging his napkin on the table*]: Oh, for God's sake, Carol. . . .

CAROL [*enthusiastically*]: No! For OUR sake, Dexter! Your prayer really made an impact on me this morning! Three years of the same old prayer . . . and then . . . zowie . . . it strikes home! Why this morning? I don't know. This was about the worst one ever . . . but, still . . . I don't know . . . but this is too much . . . I mean . . . [*She begins to laugh and to cry.*] . . . I think I'm finally beginning to see what it is all about!

[*From this point on she will become an increasingly more alive, more radiant woman; she will stand taller, speak more freely, with a different sound to her voice; DEXTER will notice this and become a bit unnerved by it at first, but he will also be attracted by it.*]

Do either of you know what I mean?

[MOTHER *is quite dumbfounded; she thinks* CAROL *has flipped; she gets up and walks around the table, walking in back of* CAROL; *she "gently" pats* CAROL *on the shoulder as she passes.*]

MOTHER: There, there, child . . . Mother Plotts understands! [*She leans over and whispers loudly into* DEXTER's *ear; her gestures indicate her belief that Carol has had it.*] Dexter . . . don't you think that we should phone. . . .

CAROL [*speaking and acting with a joyously free spirit*]: Don't worry, mother dear, I haven't flipped my lid . . . at least, not yet! [*On the "not yet" she playfully but soundly swats* MOTHER's *bottom.*]

MOTHER [*horrified, she retreats to her chair and sort of hides behind it; her voice is shaking with emotion as she asks* DEXTER]: Did you see that?

DEXTER: I HEARD it! ! [*He tries to be very stern with* CAROL, *who simply smiles at them.*] God knows I'm trying to be patient with you. . . .

CAROL: And *I* know it, my darling!

DEXTER: . . . patient and understanding. . . .

CAROL: And how I love you for it!

DEXTER: . . . but you are pushing me to the brink of . . . right to the edge of . . . physical remonstrance! But. . . . [*Still seated, he automatically reaches for*

93

his glasses and begins to stand; CAROL *reaches over and pushes him back into his chair.*]

CAROL: No, darling! Let me! ! [*She runs to his chalk-board and begins making one mark after another.*] Here's one mark! And here's another and another and another and another and another. . . . [*She very nearly fills the board; then she puts the chalk down and briskly rubs her hands together; she speaks to* MOTHER *and* DEXTER *completely without malice.*] Now . . . I hope that . . . once and for all . . . we are finished with this nonsense!

MOTHER [*closing her eyes in pain*]: Nonsense? NON-SENSE! ! [*Wide-eyed she speaks to her son*] Holy Writ! ! ! Nonsense! ! ! Did you hear that, son?

DEXTER [*deeply moved by* CAROL'S *actions and words but not quite able to accept liberation*]: Yes . . . I heard her . . . but . . . we must not be too hasty. Remember, (a) we are admonished by the Re-former to put the BEST construction on all that our neighbor says and does. . . .

MOTHER [*wildly entreating*]: But she's not your NEIGHBOR! She's your WIFE! !

DEXTER: . . . and (b) I haven't reached four-hundred-ninety yet!

MOTHER: But you're only one or two marks away! Cheat a little! [*She runs to the chalkboard, picks*

94

up the chalk, and begs DEXTER *to join her.*] What's one ittsy-bittsy mark in the vastness of eternity?

DEXTER [*trying to cool things down; he's moving toward liberation; he will begin to speak with a new voice, move more freely, and generally come alive*]: Surely you haven't forgotten that even the hairs on our heads are numbered!

MOTHER [*she takes the piece of chalk and the glove over to him*]: All right . . . all right . . . but think . . . THINK back over the years! There must be at least one item you've forgotten . . . overlooked . . . foolishly IGNORED? Why, *I* reached four-hundred-ninety during the rehearsal, wedding, and reception! Not to mention the HONEYMOON! Here . . . take up the chalk and . . . [*She struggles to get the glove on his hand; he gently but firmly resists.*]

DEXTER: Please, mother . . . don't . . . this isn't the thing to do . . . not now . . . please . . . stop it!

MOTHER: DEXTER! THIS IS MOTHER SPEAK-ING! Just one more mark and . . . [*she turns to* CAROL *menacingly*] POW! ! !

DEXTER [*he turns and walks away from* MOTHER*; he doesn't want to hurt her but at the same time he is nearly completely hooked on freedom*]: I don't know . . . I don't know what's happening exactly . . . but . . . somehow I have the feeling that . . .

95

oh, forget it . . . I don't know what I was going to say anyway. . . .

CAROL [*reading his confusion correctly*]: Here, let me help. [*She walks over to the board, picks up another piece of chalk, and is prepared to make the final mark.*] I know something that you don't know . . . something very personal . . . very private . . . something that will require every last ounce of forgiveness you have in you. . . .

MOTHER: AHA! ! ! Did you hear that? ? ? ? There's been another man! ! There still may be for all we know. Quickly now . . . make her confess . . . forgive her and then . . . POW! !

DEXTER: For Christ's sake, mother, let's listen to what . . . [*When he sees the shock on his mother's face, he begins again;* MOTHER *sits down and fans herself with her napkin.*] . . . to what she has to say!

CAROL: I'm thankful for the chance . . . to explain . . . or at least to try to explain what I want to . . . explain . . . if that makes sense. [*She walks over to the blank chalkboard.*] Have you ever wondered why I have never put a mark on my board?

MOTHER [*coming out of shock*]: Because my son has never given you cause to . . . that's why!

DEXTER [*disapprovingly*]: Mother. . . .

CAROL: No, that's NOT the reason. Although . . .

[*She looks lovingly at* DEXTER; *he tries to smile back.*] all things considered . . . he IS a pretty great guy . . . he's a WONDERFUL guy. . . .

MOTHER: You've GOT to be kidding! !

DEXTER: Mother. . . .

MOTHER: What I meant was that she didn't MEAN it!

CAROL: No, I meant it! I really did! But that's NOT the reason there are no marks here. You see . . . and this is why you must forgive me . . . I have NEVER forgiven you for the things you have done to me . . . including the things I just IMAGINED

you did. Isn't that terrible? I've not been a forgiving wife!

MOTHER: Terrible? It's HORRIBLE! ! Perfectly horrible! How do you expect your marriage to last if there's no forgiveness! Have you already forgotten your marriage counselling sessions with Pastor Johnson? [*She becomes increasingly loud as she refreshes Carol's memory.*] If he said it once he said it a MILLION times: Without forgiveness there is no love, without love there is no forgiveness, and without love and forgiveness ANY relationship is DOOMED! Any fool knows that! Ask ME! LOVE AND FORGIVENESS ARE THE HEART AND SOUL OF MARRIAGE!

CAROL: You're right! [*She walks over to Dexter's board and places her hand on it.*] But is THIS forgiveness?

MOTHER [*pacing the floor a bit; she has noticed what is happening to DEXTER and decides to win him back by using a more rational argument*]: No . . . of course it isn't! But I like to think of it as a visual aid . . . a witness . . . a symbol . . . a SIGN that points to . . . [*She walks over and places her hand on Dexter's shoulder and says proudly*] . . . a forgiving spirit!

[DEXTER *is uncomfortable; he pulls gently but decisively away from* MOTHER.]

CAROL: I'm afraid that's NOT the way I see it. Now, would you like to know HOW I see it?

MOTHER [*with a loud, supercilious smile*]: NO!

DEXTER: I would.

CAROL: It is not something . . . that is, *I* do not see it as something that says what a good guy Dexter is! I see it saying what a SLOB *I* am!

MOTHER [*with the same supercilious smile*]: Well, darling, if the shoe fits. . . .

DEXTER: Mother, I wish you wouldn't. . . .

MOTHER: Wouldn't what, dear?

DEXTER: . . . wouldn't . . . well, that you just WOULDN'T!

CAROL [*gaining time for* DEXTER]: You see, if it ONLY tells me what a slob I am, how can it be a manifestation of love?

DEXTER: You know, you're right! You're RIGHT! [*He is now a free man; he says freely and fully to his mother.*] She's right!

MOTHER [*managing a sort of smile, she replies to him, speaking through clenched teeth*]: Get hold of yourself, son . . . this is most . . . unbecoming!

DEXTER: But she's really right . . . don't you see that? Now things are beginning to fall into place. . . .

Mother: DEXTER! THIS IS MOTHER SPEAK-ING!

Dexter: . . . you know, it wasn't long after we got those boards . . . those DAMNABLE BOARDS . . . maybe it was a year . . . even less . . . when I felt . . . oh, just for a few seconds . . . but I felt that they just weren't doing what we'd thought they'd do! And as the years went by . . . each mark became a sort of DENIAL of forgiveness . . . I knew this . . . but I'd tell myself that it wasn't so . . . and then I'd find myself doing more and more stupid things . . . hoping, even praying, that some day I could be honest with myself . . . and those . . . boards! They were slowly but surely turning me into a kind of . . . dumb, stupid monster! The way I'd walk . . . and the way I'd even talk . . . it was stupid, stupid, STUPID! But I felt so trapped . . . all caged-in . . . and I kept asking myself . . . how did this mess get started . . . and . . . how could I get out of it?

Mother: DEXTER! HAVE YOU FORGOTTEN? IT WAS *I* WHO SUGGESTED THEM! FOR THAT MATTER . . . I EVEN BOUGHT THEM FOR YOU!

Dexter [*who had either forgotten or repressed the memory of their origin*]: But, WHY, mother? Why did you do it?

Mother: I don't like that TONE, young man! It's very . . . inquisitional! But I have nothing to hide

100

. . . nothing at all. I gave them to you . . . to BOTH of you . . . with the hope that they could do for your marriage what they did for mine . . . or at least what they did for a while. And then . . . [*She begins a slight sniffle and finds her handbag.*] . . . when they ceased to work for me . . . for us . . . for your father and me . . . I hoped they would do for you what they DIDN'T do for us! The idea behind them is so good . . . so biblical! But then . . . oh, it was horrible . . . your father began to CHEAT! I would . . . with all of the justification in the world . . . make a mark on my board. But then HE . . . without the slightest provocation . . . believe me, without the SLIGHTEST provocation . . . would make TWO marks on his board. [*Taking a hankie from her handbag she blows her nose loudly.*] I'd make one . . . he'd make TWO . . . one, two . . . one, two . . . one, two . . . on and on it went . . . until one day . . . one day he TURNED on me . . . [*She is crying quite freely and also dramatizing her husband's actions.*] . . . he took a . . . a CROWBAR . . . lifted it over his head . . . and with the strength of a thousand devils . . . smashed me to the ground!

DEXTER: He HIT you?

CAROL: With a CROWBAR?

MOTHER: No, no, no, sillies! Not ME! The chalk-boards! But it might just as well have been me!

Boom . . . crash . . . down they came . . . broken into a thousand pieces . . . and my heart, into a million. Right after that . . . he began taking those LONG fishing trips! [*She blows her nose one last time and then turns to* CAROL.] And now YOU want to do the same thing! Oh, you won't use a crowbar . . . but you'll destroy them . . . just wait and see! BUT . . . remember this! A blow against them is a blow against the SCRIPTURES! It's all there . . . just as plain as plain can be! Once upon a time there was a question: "How often should I forgive my neighbor . . . SEVEN times?" Then there was this answer: "No! SEVENTY times seven!" [*She turns to* DEXTER.] You should appreciate that! After all, you ARE a bookkeeper! Facts, figures, numbers, profit-loss, . . . these are the STUFF of life! And that's what the Bible's about and that's what FORGIVENESS is about!

CAROL [*gently*]: I don't know exactly how to put this but. . . .

MOTHER [*smiling through clenched teeth*]: Then don't TRY, dearie!

CAROL [*unperturbed*]: But don't you see . . . I want to . . . I HAVE to!

MOTHER: All right, all right, all right! Never let it be said of me that I have a CLOSED MIND!

CAROL: The answer you were talking about . . . the

102

seventy times seven business . . . that answer is not really an answer at all!

MOTHER [*looking at* DEXTER]: Well, at least she TRIED!

CAROL: No . . . let me finish. It's the kind of question . . . it's the kind of ANSWER that shows that the question should never have been asked in the first place! !

MOTHER: Goodness, you ARE trying . . . if you know what I mean!

CAROL: Forgiveness is NOT a numbers game!

MOTHER: Of course it's not a GAME!

CAROL: You're right! And since it's NOT a game . . . that means that you don't have to keep score!

MOTHER [*knowing that she's trapped, she immediately reverses field*]: It IS a game!

CAROL: All right, it IS a game . . . but a very PECULIAR game! If you keep score . . . everyone loses! But if you DON'T keep score . . . everyone WINS!

MOTHER [*another mighty reversal*]: It is NOT a game!

DEXTER [*slightly irritated*]: Come on, mother . . . you can't have it both ways!

MOTHER: All right, young-man-who-suddenly-knows-

more-than-his-mother-does, it is NOT a game . . .
it's a BATTLE!

CAROL [*unrelentingly*]: That's RIGHT! And by
battle . . . you mean struggle . . . pursuit . . . tenacity . . . don't you?

[*She begins stalking* MOTHER *who is in slow retreat
around the room;* DEXTER *is delighted by the turn of
events.*]

MOTHER: I suppose it could be described. . . .

CAROL: It's a matter of searching . . . and persevering
. . . and suffering . . . but always moving on, isn't
it?

MOTHER: It might resemble those. . . .

CAROL: It's give-and-take . . . retreat and advance . . .
saying YES when someone else has said NO . . . of
ducking when they swing but not swinging back
. . . of hounding them . . . tracking them . . . always
ready . . . always eager . . . reaching out . . . always
reaching out. . . .

MOTHER [*caught*]: WHAT IN THE HELL ARE
YOU TALKING ABOUT?

CAROL [*jubilantly*]: The same thing you are! FOR-
GIVENESS!

MOTHER: But I was quoting the BIBLE!

CAROL: So am I! HOSEA AND GOMER!

MOTHER: WHAT? ?

CAROL: The prophet Hosea and Gomer, his wife!

MOTHER: Gomer's a WOMAN? ? ?

CAROL [*too magnanimous to administer the coup-de-grace*]: You remember the story, don't you . . . Hosea? . . . it's a book? . . . in the Old Testament?

MOTHER: The OLD TESTAMENT! Of course, I remember that!

CAROL: Good! Then you will remember how much Hosea loved Gomer!

MOTHER [*faking it*]: Of course, I do! Why . . . it was the talk of the . . . town!

DEXTER [*lightly, since he feels that* MOTHER *is about to be turned-on too*]: Well, something like that, mother.

CAROL: But after they were married, deep trouble . . . really deep trouble began! Gomer started to . . . to. . . .

MOTHER [*who likes a good story as well as the next person does*]: STRAY a little . . . right?

CAROL: That's right!

MOTHER: Believe me, child, it's an old, old story! But it's the man . . . usually it's the man who goes looking for a little . . . hanky-panky!

105

CAROL: But THIS time it was Gomer.

MOTHER: Maybe she had her reasons . . . maybe Hosea was too busy being a PROPHET!

CAROL: Anyway, remembering their original love and still being desperately in love with her Hosea continually received her back. . . .

MOTHER: Sounds to me as though he had a guilty conscience!

DEXTER: No, mother . . . he simply LOVED her that much!

CAROL: Finally, she left him completely . . . she ran with other men . . . as a matter of fact, she finally became an out-and-out. . . .

MOTHER [*putting her fingers to her lips and closing her eyes*]: DON'T SAY IT! HINT a little if you have to . . . but don't SAY it!

CAROL: In spite of what she had become . . . in spite of what she had done to him . . . in spite of the doubts and questions and misgivings that started to become . . . chains . . . around him . . . in spite of the arguments, the judgments . . . all of the verbal assaults of his friends and family . . . in spite of EVERYTHING . . . he battled his way to his wife . . . frantically searching, desperately looking for her . . . until. . . .

MOTHER: He was pooped!

DEXTER: No!

MOTHER: He found someone else? ?

DEXTER: No, mother! Until he found HER!

MOTHER: Some find!

CAROL: That's what everyone said . . . that's even what she thought about herself! But Hosea didn't think that way!

MOTHER: That's a prophet for you! Not a normal thought in his head!

CAROL: He knew only one thing! That he loved her . . . that he wanted her . . . needed her. . . .

MOTHER: So . . . they lived happily ever after! Just as soon as they got their strength back. [CAROL *and* DEXTER *nod affirmatively*.] So what does this have to do with forgiveness?

DEXTER [*he will now show how completely liberated he has become*]: You know very good and well what it has to do with forgiveness! Please don't keep on doing the same old stupid things I did for so long!

MOTHER: DEXTER? ? ? ? MY SON! ! !

DEXTER: You're doing the very same thing I did . . . using all kinds of crazy ideas . . . and crazy actions . . . to cover up your REAL feelings!

107

MOTHER [*sitting on a chair and fanning herself with her napkin,* MOTHER *feigns some sort of spell*]: I don't know how much more of this I can stand!

DEXTER [*kneeling beside her but not giving up the attack*]: You can stand a lot more! And I'll tell you why. You want to LIVE . . . really live . . . to be happy . . . REALLY happy! You know that just as surely as I! But you're afraid . . . afraid to admit to yourself . . . just as I was . . . afraid to admit that you're not living now! And that's why we have to . . . sort of . . . sock you over the head . . . shake you up a little . . . maybe a lot. . . .

MOTHER: And I suppose that you're going to tell me that it hurts you more than it does me?

DEXTER: It doesn't hurt me one little bit, mother. . . .

MOTHER [*softly*]: Brute.

DEXTER: . . . and it won't hurt you either! It's LIFE we're dealing with, mother! LIFE!

MOTHER: Well, I hope you don't BEAT me to death in the process! [*Weakening but still resisting, she directs this cold question to* DEXTER.] And another thing . . . just whose side are you on, anyway?

DEXTER: On the side of LIFE! Which means that I'm on your side and Carol's side and on MY side! On the other hand, I am definitely NOT . . . [*He walks over to the two chalkboards.*] . . . on THIS side!

108

This is the side of DEATH! How much happiness
have these things given us? How much joy? How
have they shaped our lives? I'll tell you how . . .
they very nearly destroyed us! They tricked us into
believing that they could help us do what we didn't
think we could do by ourselves! Well . . . their days
of trickery are over . . . ended . . . finished . . .
DEAD! [*He walks haltingly toward* CAROL.] I . . .
I . . . just don't know . . . what to say.

CAROL: Neither do I.

MOTHER [*having at last got the message and cautiously making a first step back to life*]: Well, I
know what to say. It's obvious that you two have
. . . found each other . . . [*She begins the sniffles
again.*] . . . that you still love each other . . . and I
know mothers and sons continue to love one another . . . no matter what happens . . . but . . .
[*speaking to* CAROL] you . . . you could never love
me . . . not after all this!

CAROL: Oh, yes I could!

MOTHER [*blowing her nose once again*]: No you
couldn't!

CAROL: I could!

MOTHER: Couldn't!

CAROL: Yes! !

MOTHER: No! !

109

CAROL: Yes, yes, yes! ! !

MOTHER: No, no . . . [*with a weak little plaintive voice*] Yes? ? ? [CAROL *runs to her; they embrace.*]

DEXTER: This is too good to be true! I feel like . . . shouting!
MOTHER [*through tears of happiness*]: So shout!

DEXTER: WAHOOOOOOOOO! ! And . . . HIP-HIP-HURRAY! [*The women pick up the cheering but* DEXTER *stops; his face comes alive with a new idea.*] O.K. . . . O.K. . . . that's enough . . . come on, now . . . we aren't finished yet . . . I've just had the wildest idea . . . I mean, after what we've just gone through . . . I've been thinking . . . maybe we should. . . .

MOTHER [*raising her hand for silence*]: Believe it or not . . . I'm WAY ahead of you! I'm a slow starter . . . but once I get going . . . POW! [*Embarrassed by her earlier use of the word she turns to* CAROL.] Dexter . . . I thought about your father just moments after it occurred to me that Carol was right . . . right about those boards . . . right about everything else. . . . [*She walks away from the two; she is caught up in both the reproach and warmth of memory; she speaks softly.*] Oh, how I crucified him . . . our marriage . . . our love . . . on those two STUPID chalkboards! How I loved that man!

Even today . . . my happiest moments are the ones
stirred by memories of him.

CAROL [*crossing over to her*]: Then why don't you
DO something about it?

DEXTER [*joining them*]: Why don't you?

MOTHER [*walking away from them with a kind of
bitter-sweet laugh*]: Ah, my darlings, that was three
years ago . . . three long, lonely years! And I'm not
so foolish as to think he's been FISHING all this
time!

DEXTER [*pursuing her*]: But think . . . think a minute! During all these years he hasn't initiated any

legal proceedings . . . nor has he suggested that you do! And we know that he has kept the old house!

CAROL: And even if he has . . . even if the . . . situation is somewhat . . . complicated . . . remember Hosea!

MOTHER: Hosea was a MAN, my darling.

CAROL: But it is more important that he was a PERSON . . . a person who LOVED another person! And nothing . . . absolutely nothing was going to prevent the expressing . . . the living-out of that love!

MOTHER: O.K. . . . O.K. . . . but for them everything turned out . . . peachy-keen.

DEXTER: But he didn't know for SURE that he'd win. He started with no . . . automatic guarantee! I'll bet that again and again he felt that he was going to lose! But that didn't frighten him . . . it didn't frighten him so much that he quit! Sure there were risks. And the biggest risk of all was that Gomer had lost HER love for him! But he took that risk!

MOTHER [*asking* DEXTER *with a sort of desperate excitement*]: Do you think he'd take me back?

DEXTER [*quickly and joyfully*]: Yes!

MOTHER [*asking* CAROL *in the same way*]: You think there's HOPE?

112

CAROL: Yes!

MOTHER: It's worth a TRY? ? ?

DEXTER AND CAROL [*with extreme enthusiasm*]: Yes! !

[*The three are silent for a minute; each looks at the other; then the three join in a triumphant*]

ALL: YES! ! !

MOTHER: I'll do it! [*to* DEXTER] You phone the air-
port . . . [*to* CAROL] you call a taxi . . . and I'll
pack!

[*She exits hurriedly;* DEXTER *and* CAROL *look at each other for a moment; they come together a bit uncertainly; they are about to embrace when* MOTHER *bounds back in the room.*]

Where's my bible? It's not on the night stand . . .
oh, I'm so nervous!

[CAROL *quickly finds it in the kitchen and hands it to her;* MOTHER *smiles and hugs the book.*]

I simply can't go anywhere without my bible . . .
bible and credit cards . . . now THERE'S security
for the weary traveler!

[*She exits again; the couple tries to pick up where they left off but just as they touch,* MOTHER *comes in again thumbing through the bible.*]

Just where is the book of Hosea, anyway?

113

[CAROL *runs over to her and takes the book; as she is looking for Hosea,* MOTHER *speaks to* DEXTER.]

Did you know that over THREE-FOURTHS of the bible is OLD TESTAMENT?

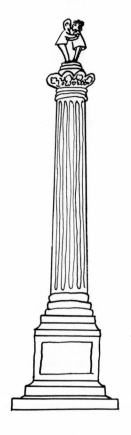

DEXTER [*delightfully impatient*]: Yes, mother . . . now run along!

[MOTHER *looks at the spot* CAROL *has found; she takes the book from her; the couple waits for a minute, expecting that* MOTHER *will return again; when she doesn't, they laugh softly and once again try for an embrace; but back bounds* MOTHER.]

MOTHER: I found it, but it's such a SHORT book! Did you know it's only TEN pages long?

DEXTER: Yes, mother . . . but think of it as a sort of . . . DIAMOND!

MOTHER [*still reading the book; she doesn't look up as she replies*]: That's right . . . a diamond it is. . . . [*She exits still reading;* CAROL *and* DEXTER *have one more go at it when back she comes.*] Dexter, promise me that first thing tomorrow you'll DESTROY those awful chalkboards!

DEXTER: I promise!

[*Just before* MOTHER *exits, she turns and sees the couple looking at her; she speaks to* DEXTER.]

MOTHER: Well, slowpoke! Hurry up and kiss her!

[*He does;* MOTHER *exits.*]

(END)

115

Throne-Prone

A farce for fellowship hall
or furnace room

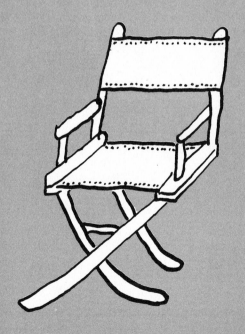

Characters

FIRST MAN: More of a fool than a clown!
SECOND MAN: More of a clown than a fool!
GAL IN THE AUDIENCE: Quite a gal!

Time

Undesignated . . . use your imagination . . . carefully.

Setting

Wherever two or three have gathered.

Throne-Prone

[*Entering church or room down center aisle, 1 grabs 2 and points toward three chairs arranged at front of nave or room.*]

1: Do you see what I see?

2 [*looks around the people, spots* GAL]: Yeh . . . and isn't she beautiful!

1 [*hits him with hat*]: No!

2: Well, I think she's beautiful!

1: That's NOT what I was talking about!

2 [*speaking to* GAL]: I still think you're beautiful!

1 [*hits with hat*]: LOOK again! [*2 looks over group.*] NOW do you see what I see?

2 [*looking at fellow*]: Yeh . . . and you're right! He IS a very distinguished looking gentleman!

1 [*hits him*]: No!

2: Well, maybe not distinguished . . . but FRIENDLY!

1: Look again!

2: Bet you a dollar that he's REAL nice to little children and puppy dogs!

1 [*moving down aisle, motions to 2 to follow*]: Will you PLEASE look!

2 [*looking at entire group*]: Well . . . everyone else looks . . . kind of ordinary! [*Speaking words of comfort*] But, don't worry! I'm SURE your mothers think that each of you is somebody REAL special!

1 [*rushes back to 2, hits him, and turns him toward chair*]: There . . . up there! Do you see what I see?

2 [*describes everything BUT the chair*]: . . . what a BEAUTIFUL SIGHT!

1 [*hits him*]: CLOSE YOUR EYES! [*Takes him by the arm, moves toward chairs.*] FOLLOW ME!

2 [*turning to people, whispers*]: I'm PEEKING!

1 [*hits with hat*]: Keep them closed . . . TIGHTLY CLOSED . . . until I tell you to open them! [*Leads to chairs.*] Now, squat down. . . .

2 [*turns to group to show them how tightly his eyes are closed*]: I'm getting a HEADACHE! [*Squats down.*]

1: NOW! What do you see?

2: Nothing!

1 [*notices that his eyes are still closed, hits him*]: DUMMY, OPEN YOUR EYES!

2 [*very quickly and loudly*]: THREE CHAIRS! I SEE THREE CHAIRS!

1: Good for you.

2: I see a papa chair and a mama chair. . . .

1 [*hits him*]: DON'T BE SO DUMB!

2: O.K. . . . I WON'T! [*Gets up and starts back toward* GAL.]

1: And just WHERE are you going?

2 [*pointing to* GAL]: Back to talk with her! That's not so dumb!

1: STOP . . . right there! [*2 stops, waves to* GAL, *then turns back toward 1.*] Now, LISTEN! [*Speaking VERY grandly.*] Chairs . . . are something . . . something VERY special . . . very special, INDEED! Each and every chair . . . be it in a peasant's cottage . . . or a king's palace . . . each chair has its own tale to tell! [*2 has been listening intently; now he bursts out laughing.*] And now what's the matter?

2: That . . . just sounded . . . funny!

1: What was so funny about it?

2 [*mocking his grand style*]: "Each chair has its own tale to tell!" [*Laughs again.*]

1: Why, pray tell, is THAT so funny?

2: It all depends on which way you spell . . . TALE! Get it?

1: And do you get . . . THIS! [*Hits him.*] NOW, listen to me! [*Walks back toward chairs.*] No . . . listen to these! Listen to these . . . CHAIRS!

122

2: Which one?

1: Any one.

2 [*walks to smallest chair, tries to listen, no luck*]: I'd better try the BIG one! [*Same bit; asks 1*] Could you . . . could you, PLEASE give me a little hint?

1: About what?

2: What it's saying! You're better at listening to chairs than I am!

1: SILENCE! AND LISTEN!

2: To . . . them? [*Points to chairs.*]

1: TO ME! [*Grandly.*] Tell me . . . do you think it ODD that there are THREE chairs here?

2 [*thinks for a moment*]: Yes . . . I do . . . [*1 reaches for his hat*] . . . I mean, NO . . . I DON'T.

1: You're right! It's not the least bit odd! In this place . . . in this context . . . the number three. . . .

2: Excuse me, please! [*Walks over to smallest chair.*]

1: Now what's wrong?

2: This chair just spoke to me! Didn't you hear it? [*Grandly.*] Pray tell, LISTEN! [*Talking with chair.*] What? No! Do you REALLY think we should? But do you think it'd work? You're right . . . what have we got to lose?

1 [*dubious but cautious*]: That chair . . . that chair is TALKING to you?

2: Can't you hear it? Here . . . [*motions him over*] . . . real close now . . . just bend down a bit . . . listen. [*As 1 follows directions, 2 boots him in rump.*] HE FELL FOR IT! [*1 turns in anger.*] The CHAIR made me do it!

1: I'm going to BREAK YOUR. . . .

2 [*backing off*]: Ask the chair . . . go ahead . . . ask the chair. . . .

1 [*to chair*]: Did you . . . [*Pauses; wonders who is fooling whom.*] O.K. . . . we'll let it pass for now . . . BUT . . . watch it from now on! As I was saying. . . .

2 [*talking to chair again*]: No . . . no, I can't do THAT! Not now! No, he wouldn't understand!

1 [*still not knowing what to make of it*]: Wouldn't understand . . . what?

2 [*still talking to chair*]: But it's . . . tempting . . . VERY tempting!

1: What is tempting?

2: You wouldn't understand.

1 [*angry*]: If you don't tell me what that chair said, I'm. . . .

2: All right, I'll tell you! [*Bursts out laughing.*] I can't!

1: If you don't. . . .

2: All right! The chair told me to tell you TO TURN THE OTHER CHEEK! Get it?

1 [*stunned*]: You have a vulgar sense of humor!

2 [*playing it big*]: SSSSHHHHH! [*Pointing to chair.*] It was the CHAIR'S idea!

1: Listen. . . .

2: To you or the chair?

1 [*motioning him over*]: Listen to ME! I'm going to let you in on a little secret! CHAIRS CAN'T TALK! [*Hits him.*]

2 [*retreating down aisle*]: But you told me to listen to it . . . to ANY chair . . . to ALL chairs!

1: What I meant was. . . .

2: So I listened . . . I believe you . . . [*Continues his retreat.*]

1: Will you stand still and listen to me?

2: I did! And look what it's gotten me!

1 [*puts hat on and stops stalking him*]: I didn't mean that chairs ACTUALLY talk! O.K.?

2: That one did!

1: IT DID NOT!

2: And it had beautiful diction!

1: IDIOT!

2: Sort of an . . . English accent! Must be a Chippendale!

1 [*stunned; then motions to him to come over; he speaks "gently"; puts arm around him*]: When I asked you to listen to that chair . . . I didn't mean LISTEN to that chair. . . .

2 [*pointing to largest chair*]: Did you mean THAT one?

1 [*reaches for hat but 2 breaks away from him*]: I was speaking metaphorically! Do you know what that means?

2: It means you were lying!

1: That's NOT what it means!

2: But that's what you were DOING!

1: Dare you even SILENTLY question my veracity!

2: I wouldn't touch your veracity with a ten-foot pole! Beg pardon? [*Turns to chair.*] He wouldn't touch it with a TWENTY-foot pole!

GAL: I wouldn't touch it with a THIRTY-foot pole!

1: SILENCE! I'm surrounded by SMALL MINDS

and GIGANTIC MOUTHS! IF it will be a consolation to your retrograde intellects, I . . . grant that initially I may have SUGGESTED that chairs DO speak; however. . . .

2: You didn't suggest it . . . you announced it . . . you proclaimed it!

1: I have the nauseous feeling that you're going to TRY to say something PROFOUND!

2: Right you are . . . so, here [*offers his hat as basin*] . . . just in case!

1 [*contemptuously*]: Pray, proceed with your . . . bleat and bray! [*Takes off hat and bows.*]

2: This is the problem! I've been listening to you, really and sincerely listening to you . . . and either I don't know what you're talking about or YOU don't know what you're talking about!

1: I KNOW what I'M talking about!

2: Then that makes it even worse! You don't BELIEVE what you're talking about! To know, to speak, but NOT to believe! . . . What a contradiction!

1 [*pause*]: Have you quite finished . . . finished spinning out that . . . that gossamer strand of NON-THOUGHT . . . or is there more?

2 [*testily*]: You bet there's MORE! [*Puts his hat on.*]

1 [*motioning toward hat*]: No . . . if there's more I may STILL need it!

GAL: Ram it down his throat!

1: SILENCE!

2: This is the problem: You understand what you say but you really don't believe it! I don't really understand what you say but I BELIEVE it! That reminds me of a line from the Confessions of Auggie Z. Gabuski. [*Pauses, trying to remember it; hand is frozen in pointed gesture.*]

1: Are you waiting for a violin accompaniment?

2: Ah, yes. Here goes: "Not to be a teacher is bad enough! Not to HAVE a teacher is worse!"

1: A teacher you want, a teacher you shall have! I shall now tell you what those three chairs represent.

2: Should I take notes?

1: You can WRITE? ? ? ?

2: Print.

1: Just listen! Ready? Those three chairs represent the TRINITY!

2: The TRINITY? ? ? ?

1: It's a doctrine of the church, biblically rooted, creedally affirmed, liturgically celebrated, and if

you don't believe it you'll BURN! [*2 bursts out laughing.*] Don't be so sacrilegious!

2: I'M NOT being sacrilegious!

1: But you're laughing at the threat of damnation!

2 [*still laughing*]: No I'm not!

1: You're laughing at the TRINITY? ? ? ?

2: I'm laughing at YOU! Those chairs don't represent the Trinity! They CAN'T!

1: Why can't they?

2: Because they're NOT the SAME size, they're NOT COEQUAL in MAJESTY, that's why!

1 [*brief pause*]: How about that? [*Quickly hits 2.*] And before you so rudely interrupted me I was going to say just THAT! Truly, you are homo ignoramus if YOU think they represent the Trinity!

2: I didn't. . . .

1: Since your attention span is but as the twinkling of an eye, you'd better take notes!

2: I did NOT say that. . . .

1: Take this down and UNDERLINE it! Those chairs do NOT represent the Trinity!

2: Then what DO they represent?

1: It's so . . . so . . . obvious!

130

2: Be careful now! I don't want to become Homo-Fingeramus-Burnatatis-for-the-Second-Timus!

1: Have you noticed that your oft attempted FLIGHT into WIT ends up so abysmally SUBTERRANEAN! [*Takes him by arm.*] Come with me! [*Turns to* GAL.] YOU . . . stay THERE! [*Walking up aisle.*] Those chairs represent . . . the Biblical Communications System! One is Command Central; the other is Decoding-Interpretation; the last is Obedient-Action. Now . . . sit in the chair [*superciliously*] APPROPRIATE to your . . . station! [*2 moves directly to largest chair.*] THAT'S NOT YOURS!

2 [*laughs good-naturedly*]: I didn't think so. [*Sits in smallest chair.*] Or is this YOUR chair?

1 [*icily*]: No!

GAL: Give him the ELECTRIC CHAIR!

1: You two are genuine, fourteen-karat medical wonders! Your ability to bear the burden of your mountainous stupidity is nothing short of miraculous!

2: Sure, we're dumb! Sure, we've got lots to learn. So TEACH us! Be our teacher!

GAL: Yeh, Teach . . . I'd like to give you an apple! Rotten . . . and right between the eyes!

1: Were I to attempt to describe your ignorance . . . its breadth, its depth. . . .

131

2: That's what we DON'T need! Don't humiliate us! TEACH us!

1: Why not ask me to do something easy . . . like RAISE THE DEAD!

GAL: Just drop dead!

2: Answer me this . . . why aren't you ANGERED by our ignorance?

1: Angered? ? ? ? I'm positively LIVID with rage!

2: But you're NOT! If you were REALLY angry you'd do one of two things: eradicate our ignorance OR eradicate us!

1: That second option . . . you know, it's . . . it's not all that bad.

2: But you are NOT angered by our ignorance. You are DELIGHTED by it!

1: I'm WHAT?

2: Delighted by it! Keep us here and keep us dumb and . . . wow . . . are you ever happy! That REALLY makes you MISTER BIG!

1 [pause]: Very well! Engarde. I shall now proceed to SLAY YOUR ignorance. But hers . . . well, my reverence for primitive forms of life is such that I cannot bring myself to slay the last of . . . the NEANDERTHALS!

GAL: I'd like to crease your skull with the shin bone of a brontosaurus!

1 [*to 2*]: Shall WE proceed? Now, I'll take my place . . . [*Walks toward chairs and has to fight himself and his desire to sit in largest chair; takes middle-size.*]

2 [*knowing the meaning of the hesitation*]: Mighty TEMPTING, wasn't it?

1: I was merely . . . REVERENCING that chair, O.K.?

GAL: Liar!

1 [*imploring 2*]: Can't you do something with her?

2 [*flustered*]: Well . . . I'm not sure . . . what I could do. . . .

GAL: Come on back, honey! We'll think of something!

2 [*quickly changing subject*]: So start interpreting . . . or decoding . . . or whatever it is you do!

1: Interpreting?

2: Yeh, the command . . . decode the command.

1: I'm trying to but you won't listen to the command!

2: I'm listening FOR the command, I really am! Now let's sit very quietly and listen!

1: Very well, you do that! [*Very grandly.*] Listen!

The word of command is this: You have heard that it was written. . . .

2: WAIT A MINUTE!

1: No, YOU wait a minute!

2: I am waiting . . . FOR THE COMMAND!

1: And you're GETTING it. . . .

2: But YOU'RE speaking!

1: Of course, I'M speaking!

2: But you said that [*points to largest chair*] THERE is the word of command!

1: That's right!

2: And you MEAN it?

1: Of course I mean it!

2: You're NOT pretending to mean it this time?

1: I ALWAYS mean what I say!

2: And you are JUST the interpreter, the decoder, right?

1: I would not use the word "JUST" . . . it's so . . . so. . . .

GAL: ACCURATE?

2: Since you are, by your own admission, NOT the COMMANDER, let's all listen to THAT. [*Points to largest chair again.*]

1: I told you once, I've told you twice, I'LL tell you THRICE! Chairs DON'T talk!

2: I heard them!

1: You did not! You . . . you are the pretender, not I! You breathe and snort deceit!

2 [*good natured laugh*]: O.K. . . . you're right . . . that chair DIDN'T speak to me. . . .

1: Aha!

2: . . . I was only pretending!

1: Aha!

2: Had you worried though, didn't I?

GAL: I HEARD THE CHAIR!

BOTH 1 AND 2: You did? ? ? ? ! !

GAL [*laughing too*]: Just kidding! Carry on!

1 [*speaking to 2 but pointing to* GAL]: Yon . . . HAG is ready! Are you?

GAL: Sticks and stones may break. . . .

1: SILENCE!

GAL [*quickly*]: But names can never hurt me!

1 [*to 2*]: Now you listen, and you listen good! The word of command is this! [*Pauses; big histrionics.*] You have heard that it was written. . . .

2: Stop, wait, cease, and desist! ! That's NOT. . . .

1: What in the name of my Aunt Frieda's cat do you want me to do? ? ? ?

2: Interpret or decode but DON'T command!

1: But FIRST we must HEAR that command!

2: I'm waiting!

1: So LISTEN!

2: NOT TO YOU! You're sitting there . . . NOT [*pointing to largest chair*] THERE!

1: I could SCREAM!

GAL: Male chauvinist PIG!

1 [*leaps from his chair and sits in largest chair; 2 is stunned*]: NOW WILL YOU LISTEN TO THE WORD OF COMMAND? DON'T ANSWER! LISTEN! I'M TIRED OF YOUR SILLY GAMES! SICK OF YOUR UNRELENTING PRETENSE! [*2 takes off his hat.*] NAUSEATED BY YOUR EMPTY WORDS, YOUR EMPTY HEAD, AND YOUR EMPTY SOUL! YOU WANT TO HEAR THE WORD OF COMMAND? THEN LISTEN! I'VE TOLERATED YOUR IMPUDENCE LONG ENOUGH! YOU CANNOT WITH IMPUNITY TRIVIALIZE THE HOLY OF HOLIES! GOD WILL NOT BE THUS MOCKED! TEMPT ME NO FURTHER LEST I RISE UP IN HOLY WRATH AND SMITE YOU AND YOUR. . . .

137

2 [*lunging at 1, flaying him with his hat*]: Stop it, stop it, stop it! That's what I mean! [*He has pushed 1 back into middle-size chair.*] This is YOUR chair. Not this one! Understand?

1: You . . . you STRUCK me!

2: You are NOT God!

1: You struck me!

2: You are an INTERPRETER!

1: You struck me!

2: You cannot, DARE not command! If you aren't happy as an interpreter, fine! I think we can find another LITTLE chair for you. . . .

1: You struck me!

GAL: Hit 'im again harder, harder!

2: Or . . . you can take my chair . . . and I'll. . . .

1: Don't you DARE touch me again!

2: . . . and I'll take a fling at interpreting! Come on now . . . I'll take your chair!

1: YOU'LL WHAT? ? ? ?

2: Someone has got to do the job. . . .

1: JOB? ? ? ? Out! Oaf! It's not a JOB! It's a CALL-ING!

138

2: Call it what you will . . . I'LL DO it! Come on . . . you can have MY chair . . . and I'll. . . .

1: That impiety would cost you your LIFE! A thousand bolts of lightning would consume you.

2: You really think so?

1: I KNOW so!

2: How much do you wanna bet?

1: But you'll be KILLED!

2 [*pointing to largest chair*]: But you sat there . . . and you're no more an ash now than before!

1: But I have a CALLING!

GAL: There are a couple of choice things I'd like to call you. . . .

1: SILENCE!

2: Well . . . [*Returns to little chair.*] we've got us a REAL problem haven't we? A really big problem! [*Sighs, rubs eyes, is exhausted.*] I . . . I don't know . . . I just don't know if I can handle it. [*Long pause.*]

1 [*new role*]: Would you like to talk about it?

2: Yes . . . as a matter of fact I would. [*Slowly begins stretching out on his little chair, slowly transforming it into a couch.*] You see. . . .

1: Yes?

2: You see . . . [*long pause*] . . . well, it's all very complicated.

1: Complicated?

2: Yes . . . but in a . . . simple sort of way.

1: Simple, eh?

2: Well, not . . . TOO simple.

1: Sort of . . . semi-simple?

2 [*pause*]: No.

1: No?

2: No.

1: Oh?

2: It's more . . . mini-simple.

1: You mean. . . .

2: Yes, that's right. It's all . . . very, very complicated.

1: And that . . . frightens you?

2: FRIGHTENS me? ? ? ?

1: I meant to say . . . bothers. Does it BOTHER you?

2: Does WHAT bother me?

1: That . . . that life is so . . . complicated.

2: No.

1: IT DOESN'T? ? ? ?

2: Doesn't what?

1: Bother you that life is so complicated?

2: You've noticed that too, eh?

1: Ah, yes . . . yes, indeed. Life is complicated . . . rotten and complicated.

2 [*sitting up in his chair; slowly reversing roles*]: Would you like to talk about it?

1: Rotten and complicated . . . and cruel. Yes . . . [*sliding down in his chair*]. . . .

2: Yes?

1: I'd like to talk about it. You see, when I was just a little boy . . . oh, maybe five or six years old . . . I had a . . . a. . . . [*Pause.*]

2: You had a. . . .

1: I . . . I don't want to talk about it.

2 [*pause*]: It . . . it might be helpful to you if you would.

1: You'd . . . you'd laugh.

2: No . . . I wouldn't laugh.

1: Yes you would.

2: I never laugh AT people.

1: Never?

2: Never.

1: You PROMISE you won't laugh?

2: I promise.

1: When I was just a little boy . . . eleven or twelve years old. . . .

2: Yes?

1 [*rushing, on verge of tears*]: I . . . I had a big . . . Raggedy-Ann doll. . . .

2 [*bursts out laughing*]: You had a what?

1 [*coming out of it and noticing the reversal*]: WHAT IN THE NAME OF SENSE ARE YOU DOING? YOU'RE THE ONE WHO'S FRIGHTENED BY LIFE, NOT I. YOU'RE TERRIFIED OF COMPLICATIONS, NOT I. ALL I'M TRYING TO DO IS CALM YOU DOWN! [*2 has closed his eyes and begins to snore.*] OH, YOU'RE CUTE . . . SO VERY, VERY CUTE!

2 [*eyes still closed*]: Would you like to talk about it?

1 [*walking around in rage*]: You . . . you are the most loathsome creature I have ever met! I would like to. . . .

2 [*jumps up and points to largest chair*]: YOU WOULD LIKE TO SIT IN THAT CHAIR AND YOU'RE ANGRY AT ME BECAUSE I WON'T LET YOU!

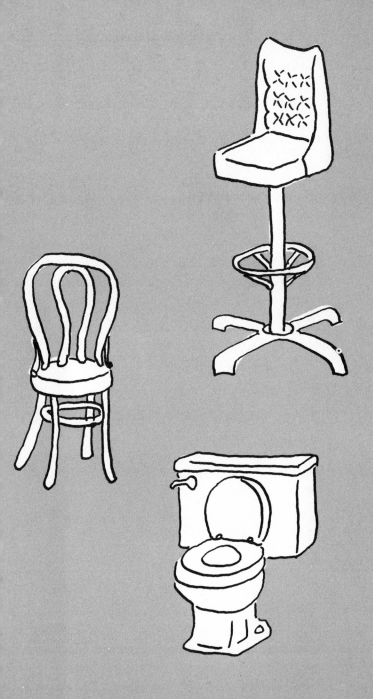

1: YOU won't let me? ? ? ? ? Well, just watch THIS! [*He stomps to chair, looks contemptuously at 2, and just as he begins to sit, 2 shouts at him.*]

2: DON'T DO THAT! [*1 pauses.*] A MILLION BOLTS OF LIGHTNING MIGHT, JUST MIGHT, REDUCE YOU TO ESSENCE OF ASH!

1 [*smiles sardonically and returns to his regular chair*]: You . . . you are a . . . well, let me put it this way: Does it bother you that your father and mother never MARRIED?

2 [*laughs good naturedly*]: Hey, that's pretty good! You know, you're really not such a bad sort after all. That was . . . kind of clever . . . witty.

1 [*duly buttered up*]: Well, thank you. . . .

2: BUT! ! [*Pointing to largest chair*] That is a NO-NO! If it is wrong for me to try to sit in my chair AND yours, it is equally wrong of you to occupy [*pointing to largest chair*] THAT one. Your CALL places you there . . . NOT THERE!

1: Are you suggesting that I have some . . . some LATENT desire to be GOD?

2: No! The desire is NOT latent!

1: You insolent puppy! Oh, if I were ON-LY in charge of those lightning bolts, I'd. . . .

2: You see, that's EXACTLY what I mean! I know you better than you know yourself!

1: A little knowledge is a dangerous thing!

2: It is?

1: Horribly dangerous!

2: Would you like to talk about it?

1: You are just too dumb to know how dangerous it is to be dumb!

2: You're right! It IS foolish, dangerously foolish of me to think that I could sit in two chairs!

1: Well, miracle of miracles! The blithering idiot is SLOWLY losing some of his . . . BLITHER!

GAL: I'd like to wither your blither with a . . . with a. . . .

1: With a WHAT?

GAL: With a. . . .

1: All right, dearie, let's hear it . . . I'm waiting. You'd like to "wither my blither with a. . . ."

GAL: HATCHET!

1: Were I to add together BOTH your I.Q.'s the total sum would be on the dismal side of ZERO!

2: At least I have brains enough to know that this is

MY chair, that is yours, and THAT ONE . . . well, I know it's NOT yours!

1: Imbecile, did I say it was?

2: No, but you're trying to get it . . . through squatter's rights!

1: Squatter's rights? ? ? ?

GAL: I saw you put your big fat squatter right on it!

2: You COVET that chair!

1: Well, now . . . let him or [*looking at* GAL] . . . IT . . . among you who has NOT coveted that chair, cast the first stone!

2: You're right! I do covet that chair! [*Gets up and moves over to largest chair and sits in it.*] Ah, you're right! This feels REAL good.

1 [*horror stricken*]: You're . . . you're. . . .

2 [*Jehovah-like*]: AND TAKE OFF YOUR HAT IN MY PRESENCE. GAZE NOT ON MY COUNTENANCE! KNEEL IN MY PRESENCE! MURMUR NOT A WORD! KNOW THAT I COULD WITH PERFECT JUSTICE . . . ZAP YOU! [*Returns to former self.*] Oh, yeh, this is great! You know what? This will KILL you. I feel . . . I feel strangely AT HOME here! Very, VERY comfortable! And that's my GUT-LEVEL reaction! How's it grab you?

1 [*virtually speechless*]: You . . . you are the abomination of abominations! To usurp the throne is sacrilege sufficient! But to SAY . . . nay . . . to DECLARE that it is your . . . your NATURAL OFFICE is. . . .

2: Not nice?

1: Lucifer made the same claim and LOOK what happened to him! [*2 whistles and gestures a plane in tailspin.*] Right on!

2: Now, look it . . . I sit in this chair and what happens to me? I . . . just feel comfortable . . . strangely at home. BUT . . . you sit here and what happens? For one thing, you become pompous! Well, that really doesn't bother me. BUT you ALSO become angry, bitter, and brutal!

1: I DO NOT!

2: I sit here and in some strange way . . . remember who I am. You sit here and FORGET who you are!

1: I AM THE INTERPRETER!

2: NOT THE COMMANDER!

1: Yes, but I read the Scriptures!

2: So do I!

1: NOT in Greek or Hebrew!

2: And NOT in Sanscrit or Swahili or POLISH!

1: I know the great teachers of the faith! Peter, Paul, Augustine, Luther, Calvin, AND Rudolph Klotz!

GAL: Mother pin a rose on you!

2: All of whom were INTERPRETERS, right?

1 [*after very long speechless pause*]: Why don't you like me?

2 [*taken aback by question*]: Like you? Well . . . I don't exactly. . . .

1: Be honest now. You don't like me, do you?

2: Well, it's true . . . I . . . I wouldn't want my sister to MARRY you . . . but that doesn't mean I dislike you . . . exactly.

1 [*shouting*]: IT'S IMPERATIVE THAT WE BECOME FRIENDS!

2: Imperative?

1 [*calming down*]: I mean . . . I'd LIKE to be your friend.

2: Well . . . golly, I guess a guy can never have TOO many friends.

1: We should spend some time together . . . we've lots of things to talk about . . . sort out.

2: Yeh, well . . . that sounds O.K. . . .

1: Good! You know, there's a quiet little Retreat

Center just down the road [*Walks over and puts arm on 2's shoulder.*]. . . .

2: Retreat Center? That's not exactly NEUTRAL territory!

1: You don't TRUST me?

2: Trust? Try some other word.

1: You DON'T trust me!

2: I'd LIKE to trust you!

1: So . . . when can we begin . . . WHERE can we begin?

GAL: AT THE PUB!

1: THAT'S neutral territory?

2: It's at least a BEGINNING!

GAL: First you bend your elbows
              And then you bend your knees!
              Ein prost then Pater noster
              And soon you're thick as fleas!

BOTH 1 AND 2: WHY NOT? ? ? ?

1: But first. . . . [*Gestures to his chair and 2's; he gallantly picks up his chair and places it in the largest; 2 places his on top; both shake hands and begin walking down the aisle; 1 calls out to* GAL.] Come along, little lady, I can tell you've worked up quite a thirst!

149

GAL: Who's buying?

1: I am!

GAL: Then I'm NOT going.

2: I'M buying!

GAL [*gets up and joins them*]: Then let's GO! Last one there is . . . ORDAINED!

(END)

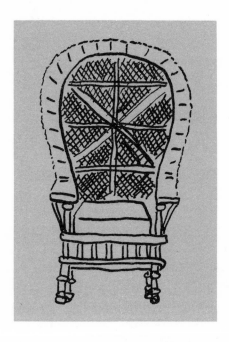

150